CHINA
TOWN
KITCHEN

CHINA TOWN KITCHEN

From Noodles to Nuoc Cham

Delicious Dishes from Southeast Asian Ingredients

LIZZIE MABBOTT

An Hachette UK Company
www.hachette.co.uk

First published in Great Britain in 2015 by
Mitchell Beazley, a division of Octopus Publishing Group Ltd
Endeavour House
189 Shaftesbury Avenue
London WC2H 8JY
www.octopusbooks.co.uk

ISBN 978 1 84533 961 6

A CIP catalogue record for this book is available from the British Library.

Printed and bound in China

10 9 8 7 6 5 4 3 2 1

Publishing Director Stephanie Jackson
Senior Editor Sybella Stephens
Copy Editor Jo Richardson
Deputy Art Director & Designer Yasia Williams-Leedham
Illustrator Abigail Read
Photographer David Munns
Prop Stylist & Art Director Tabitha Hawkins
Home Economist Annie Rigg
Senior Production Manager Peter Hunt

CONTENTS

INTRODUCTION

Of half Chinese and half English parentage, I grew up in Hong Kong. It's a smelly, noisy and hectic city; the name translates rather romantically as 'fragrant harbour' – really, it is anything but. Most people who visit are completely overwhelmed by it. My childhood memories are tinged with the smell of food cooking street-side, mingled with traffic fumes and garbage. Add to this heady mix the whiff of petrol from the sampans and ferries gathering in said harbour, and they blend together to make an unforgettable atmosphere. In summer, the temperatures reach a high of 35°C (95°F) with humidity only known in sub-tropical countries; when visiting recently, as my hair turned into a bird's nest, I wondered how I coped. I imagine I was less concerned about how I looked back then.

Growing up, some of my peers lived a more sterile life in townhouses in exclusive areas, their parents being ex-pats sent by their employers with expense accounts to pay the sky-high rents. When visiting, I was fascinated by the stairs they actually had in their houses. We were the opposite; my father moved to Hong Kong in the early '80s on a whim and my mother was a local. We lived just about everywhere on Hong Kong Island – from a relaxed, beachside apartment in the touristy Stanley area, to high-rise housing estates in Aberdeen and most memorably the grimy confines of Causeway Bay. My daily trip to school involved negotiating the dank, dark corridors of our apartment block, lit by flickering fluorescent lights, and then waiting at the bus stop early in the morning while butchers ferried carcasses down the streets, wearing them like a grotesque piggyback.

Although Hong Kong was a bustling place, it was safe on the streets and from a young age I was given absolute freedom of it. Outdoors in the stifling heat just off the busy roads, men and young students alike would sit on plastic chairs slurping up noodles, steam rising to their faces. Vendors sold fish balls on sticks, the charcoal enticing you in, finishing them with a lick of curry sauce and a shake of chilli powder while you impatiently waited for them to be cool enough to eat. We would spend weekends getting on the ferry to Lamma Island to gorge on seafood, and I would pretend to be the hand of God as I gleefully picked out a doomed fish from the tank to be freshly dispatched for our lunch. My favourite dish was clams freshly stir-fried with black beans, garlic and chilli. I'd suck the flesh out of one half of the shells, sauce dribbling down my face and staining my T-shirt. Like most Chinese kids, we were brought up to be ultimate eaters, and not much made us squeamish.

Roadside shacks with corrugated-iron roofs, dark and noisy within, served French toast piled high on melamine plates – bread dipped in egg and deep-fried, a jug of golden syrup to pour over it at the table. At lunchtimes, businessmen would fling their ties over their shoulders while ladies folded napkins on to their laps to come away pristine and ready to go back to work. Strong tea made with sweet evaporated milk and then poured at a height to make a frothy top was how I learned to love caffeine.

Strip-lit cafés served junky instant noodles in salty broth, perhaps topped with a slice of fried SPAM, or a fried egg nestling on top. I still love SPAM, as you might come to realize. The best chicken you could eat came from places like this, fried with a drizzle of soy sauce and a slick of ginger and spring onion oil. It was for everyone – the poor, the wealthy. Everyone in Hong Kong had a passion for food. This wasn't just food you'd eat as a guilty pleasure; it was part of Hong Kong culture.

Sundays were spent in cavernous, brightly lit restaurants for the family dim sum brunch. Back then, my grandfather would arrive first, far earlier than everyone else, to nab the best table. He'd read the paper, sip tea and snack on a few spring rolls while our family gathered in dribs and drabs, noisily greeting each other and settling into their seats. Trolleys full of steamers wheeled past, their drivers calling out their contents. I would poke my head inquisitively in their direction and the ladies pushing them would cock a lid so that I could steal a glimpse of inside. I'd gaze wide-eyed, nose wrinkled as elder aunties would choose a braised chicken's foot from the steamer for their bowl, only to suck all the skin off the bones and then delicately but deliberately spit all the bones out on to the tablecloth, chopsticks sometimes guiding the way. It was a real art, honed by many years of practice and one I haven't yet mastered but perhaps something to look forward to in later life. The lazy Susan piled high with dishes constantly revolved and I soon learned not to spin it before my time; a sharp rap on the knuckles with a chopstick was all it took.

My grandmother lived with us for many of my formative years. She'd get us out of bed in the morning with a devastating wrench of the duvet cover, tell us off when my sister and I fought and take us for secret snacks at McDonald's. If ever we expressed a particular fondness for an after-school snack, that was it; it would be ours every day until we pleaded for something new. Often we'd go to the wet markets with her. The people manning the stalls were all familiar friends and they'd coo over my sister and ruffle my hair, teasing me for looking like a boy with my bowl haircut (thanks Mum). My grandmother would wander from stall to stall, selecting the fresh vegetables and picking up still-wriggling fish to inspect their freshness. A finger pointed at a particular chicken pacing nervously in a cage would mean the end for it; she always instructed me to look away when it was dealt with, and I disobeyed only once. The chicken soup that evening was difficult to swallow.

In the kitchen, though, we were often shooed away. Hong Kong kitchens are never spacious – there were always pots and pans bubbling away, a wok sizzling, a rice cooker steaming. We were relegated to the living room to be amused by the television. I learned no culinary skills from my grandmother, much to my dismay, but what was imparted to me was the joy of eating.

I moved to the UK when I was 13 and I soon realized that the food I grew up with was unobtainable in rural Suffolk. My poor mother was left to fend for herself in a foreign country with two children while my father tied up all the paperwork back in Hong Kong, and not being much of a cook herself and rather homesick too, we ate a lot of Chinese takeaway. We were aghast by the nuclear-orange sweet and sour chicken, and repulsed by the sickly-sweet crispy chilli beef, but at least some of the noodle dishes were passable and others that were served with rice. I threw myself into British life. Those dishes now hold a special place in my heart.

By the time I left home at 18 and moved to London, I really did miss the meals of my childhood. Nostalgic flashbacks would come unbidden. On some winter days, I wouldn't be able to get the thought of tender, melting beef brisket slow-braised with star anise and cinnamon out of my head. Other times I actively craved that sunshine-yellow egg custard tart; I'd positively drool over the memory of still-warm flaky pastry, the just-set custard dissolving in my mouth. It was unbearable.

So I began researching recipes for those dishes I missed, from comforting home-style cooking to fancier restaurant dishes. This took me to the heart of Chinatown, and tentatively I studied labels on jars, bought odd-looking ingredients on a whim and had to look up how on earth I'd use them once I got home. It was an experimental and lengthy process, but I fell in love with the Asian supermarkets. Not only did they provide me with access to delicious food, each trip was a trip down memory lane – I could pick up particular brands and squeal 'I remember this!'

I started my blog, Hollow Legs, in March 2008 so that I'd be able to document the recipes I was discovering. The name came from a nickname my parents gave me for my insatiable appetite (commonly known as greediness). I trawled forums, blogs, recipe sites and the like to get an idea of the recipes I was after so that I could experiment with them all, borrowing ideas from some and embellishing others with my own touches – often, more chilli was added to spicy dishes, more vinegar to sour. My taste buds seem to love those flavours the most. Slowly but surely I learned to cook. It was very much trial and error – a LOT of error, aided by some cursing – but the Internet is a wonderful thing. YouTube videos showed me various cooking techniques, while other blogs with step-by-step instructions or pictures helped me out with the rest. The Asians are a keen bunch, not only loving their food but having an incredible desire to share their recipes.

Over time, I grew more adventurous; I branched out into other cuisines such as Korean, Japanese and Thai. Though I admire Western cookery and I am seriously fiendish for pasta, it never quite took me as much as Asian food did, and still does. It fascinates me; bright, perky, in-your-face flavours dominate the Asian cuisines, and they take no prisoners. Several trips to Thailand, Malaysia and Singapore cemented this fascination, while the Asian supermarkets, be it in Chinatown or online, enabled me to make the recipes I loved the most at home in the UK.

This book is a guide to the Asian supermarket and the treasures you can find within. The supermarkets themselves are often described as intimidating, daunting or confusing. They're usually big spaces, packed with packets, jars, tins and spices in varying degrees of comprehensibility. My hope is that in sharing the main attributes of common ingredients via the recipes here, the intimidation will lessen and you will gain confidence in Asian food, as I did.

This isn't supposed to be an educational tome, tangled in the authenticity of cuisines. There are some classic recipes remade to my take in here, but you'll also find that I've downright rejected authenticity in a couple of the recipes to make way for what tastes good – that's what it's all about, isn't it? It's what I hope to be a fun, accessible book that showcases ingredients used often in Asian cookery. Each chapter has a list and summary of things you might find in each aisle – a sort of index, so that after a quick glance for reference you can find what you're looking for more easily or which category something belongs in.

I can't say that after cooking from this book that you will become an expert in Asian cuisine (is anyone, really?), but that isn't really my intention either. What I hope for is that you'll feel the excitement I get when I walk into an Asian supermarket; a sense of flavoursome possibility, and a feeling of adventure in experimenting with everything inside them.

BASIC EQUIPMENT

WOK & LID

The humble wok is probably the most important piece of equipment in the Asian kitchen. Don't bother with the expensive fancy nonstick coated types; all you need is a flat-bottomed stainless steel one that you can buy from most Asian supermarkets, some cooking oil and a bit of time to make it nonstick.

Firstly, open all the doors and windows of your kitchen, as this can get a little smoky. Use a brush or a sponge with plenty of soapy water and give the wok a good scrub, to remove the machine oil residue. Dry the wok and then place it on the hob over the highest heat. Move the wok around so that the heat reaches the sides all over – you will see it will start changing colour. Add 3–4 tablespoons of vegetable oil to the wok and swirl it around carefully, using a piece of kitchen paper to reach the more difficult places. Continue heating like this for another minute or two, then take off the heat and wipe any residual oil out. Leave to cool for 10 minutes, then place back on the heat with another tablespoon of oil and repeat the process until you have a uniform brown/black patina developing.

Don't stir-fry any starches, such as rice or noodles, until you have used the wok a few more times and have really developed that patina further. After you have used your wok, clean it with water – no soap or detergent – and a soft brush, then place back on the heat to dry it, wipe it round with a little cooking oil and leave to cool. This prevents it from rusting. You soon get into the habit.

DOLSOT

A dolsot is a traditional Korean granite stone bowl, used for dishes such as bibimbap (rice topped with ingredients, followed by a raw egg that cooks in the residual heat of the bowl – most prized for the crispy rice that forms at the bottom of the bowl). When heated on the stove or in the oven, the granite retains the heat well, and so cooks the dish more effectively. The dolsot should be heated gradually to avoid cracking the bowl.

CHINESE CLAY POTS

These usually come in various sizes with a lid. They should be soaked overnight in a sink full of water before their first use, and like the dolsot, should be heated gradually after being soaked in cold water for 15 minutes first. The Chinese believe that cooking in clay pots give the dish a distinct flavour and keeps the nutrients within. Claypots are mainly used for one pot dishes, such as Bo Kho or Braised Chicken, Broccoli and Shiitake Mushrooms.

RICE COOKER

You don't have to have one of these, but it's worth it if you are going to be cooking a lot of Asian food. It frees up hob space, you don't have to worry about anything bubbling over and it keeps rice warm for as long as you like.

STEAMER

Either a metal steamer insert for a saucepan or a bamboo steamer are ideal. A metal steamer insert for the wok is also great for steaming larger ingredients.

CLEAVER

A simple chopping cleaver from the Asian supermarket is great for when you need to chop through meat or poultry bones or carcasses. Otherwise, a chef's knife has served me well.

COOKING CHOPSTICKS

These are particularly good for moving delicate ingredients around, far more so than tongs.

METAL SPATULA

As well as cooking chopsticks, a metal spatula is handy for moving food around at high heat.

CHOPPING BOARD

A large, sturdy wooden chopping board is a good idea; Asian cooking often involves a lot of chopping of different items, and for efficiency I like to have all my ingredients for cooking lined up and ready to go.

PESTLE & MORTAR

A sturdy pestle and mortar is very handy for Asian food. They are useful to make garlic or ginger pastes, or dressings. Look for a high-sided granite one; they're best for keeping ingredients in one place, so you can go to town with the pestling. You can use a mini chopper, but many say a curry paste made by hand is far superior.

BASIC INGREDIENTS

Loading up with supplies for an Asian kitchen storecupboard can be a bit daunting, but once you have got these items in store, it means that for each individual recipe you will only need to pick up fresh ingredients and a flavouring or two.

LIGHT SOY SAUCE

This is the most commonly used seasoning in Japanese and Chinese dishes, its primary function being to add salt to dishes. It's worth buying the best quality you can, as it's used so often and there is a real difference in quality. I favour Pearl River Bridge Premium Deluxe. Tamari is a gluten-free alternative for coeliacs.

DARK SOY SAUCE

This soy sauce is used sparingly, often for a hint of colour and a caramel-like depth of flavour, so you can start off with a smaller bottle.

OYSTER SAUCE

Thick, glossy and slightly sweet, oyster sauce is frequently used to give sauces body, or to season vegetables. When choosing which brand to buy, look for the highest percentage of oyster extract in the ingredients.

FISH SAUCE

Mostly used in Thai, Cambodian, Laotian, Filipino and Vietnamese food, fish sauce is an amber-coloured liquid that is fermented with salt. It is often used to cook with, but is also used in dressings and dipping sauces. The quality of different fish sauce brands varies; I prefer Three Crabs for a more subtle and smooth flavour.

CHINKIANG BLACK VINEGAR

Used mostly in Southern Chinese dishes, Chinkiang black vinegar has a smoky flavour with a hint of sweetness. It's usually added to a dish at the end of cooking to preserve its delicacy, and is also used for dipping sauces and marinades.

RICE VINEGAR

Clear and white, rice vinegar is much stronger and more acidic than black vinegar, though still more mellow than Western counterparts.

RICE WINES

Shaoxing rice wine is used the most in this book, but it's also worth picking up some cooking sake if you come across it, for Japanese dishes.

SESAME OIL

Toasted sesame oil is frequently used to flavour a dish, rather than to cook things in. The anomaly is when it comes to Korean food, where sesame oil is often used to cook with but usually untoasted for a milder flavour. If you don't want to buy both, go for toasted and mix it with a little vegetable oil when preparing Korean dishes.

CHILLI OIL

Make your own by heating chilli flakes in vegetable or groundnut oil. You can also grind together dried chillies, salt and garlic with a pestle and mortar, then slowly cook the mix in vegetable oil until red hued and infused. Alternatively, there are lots of great chilli oils you can buy ready made. I like jars with sediment in, for extra kick, and I always check the label for ones without MSG (monosodium glutamate – see page 16) or E numbers.

FRAGRANT JASMINE RICE

You can use basmati, you can use brown, but white fragrant jasmine rice is the most commonly used rice in Asian cookery. If you're serious about Asian food, I'd urge you to get a rice cooker (see page 11). But otherwise, follow the cooking method on page 47.

GINGER, GARLIC & SPRING ONIONS

I am never without these three ingredients, often considered to be the holy trinity of Chinese cooking, and garlic is used liberally throughout Asia. So it's worth keeping these items on hand at all times.

WHITE PEPPER

You can buy whole white peppercorns, but the ground stuff is pungent too and much easier to handle.

COOKING OIL

A lot of my recipes start off with 'Heat the oil in a wok'. My oil of choice is vegetable or sunflower oil; olive oil, though healthier, is too flavoursome for Asian cooking, and peanut or groundnut oil, which many traditional cooks use, goes rancid comparatively quickly.

CORNFLOUR & POTATO STARCH

These are used a lot in marinades and to thicken sauces. While most of the time the two are interchangeable, potato starch crisps up better for deep-fried food.

DRIED SHIITAKE MUSHROOMS

These are often added to dishes or used as a flavouring. Always buy them whole and look for those with a white fissured flower pattern on the cap; these are more expensive, but better quality. To use, soak in water overnight for the best flavour, but if you're in a rush, you can soak them in boiling water for 30 minutes without too much detriment. Always discard the stem before using, and you can strain the mushroom water to use as a stock.

CHAPTER

SAUCES & CONDIMENTS

SAUCES & CONDIMENTS

Many Asian sauces and condiments head for one objective; Japanese miso paste, Sichuan chilli bean paste and Korean doenjang and gochujang are all made by fermenting soya beans in order to build a base layer of that fifth taste that accompanies the other four of sweet, salty, bitter and sour – umami. The best way to describe it is deeply savoury; yes, it's salty, but it's more than that. It's what makes your dish go from tasting good to tasting excellent. MSG (monosodium glutamate), which is now a dirty word, is chemically manufactured umami, but this chemical compound is naturally occurring in foods like tomatoes, mushrooms and Parmesan cheese. Anchovies have a high level of umami too, which goes a little way to understanding the liberal uses of fish sauce, shrimp sauce and prawn paste in many cuisines. It is, in the simplest sense, deliciousness.

In an ideal world, we would be able to make everything we eat completely from scratch, without E numbers and preservatives, but in Asian cooking life is just too short to ferment your own soya beans and make your own soy sauce. All the following sauces and condiments are available in Asian supermarkets. Some brands are of higher quality than others, and when I'm shopping for them I tend to check the labels, as some have more E numbers than others.

I'm sure there are many soya bean-based condiments, but the following are the ones that I've found to be most commonly available in my Asian supermarket snoopings, and those I use the most.

GOCHUJANG

This is Korean chilli paste, made by fermenting soya beans with chilli, salt and glutinous (sticky) rice in the sun. Often sold in a red plastic tub, the paste is smooth, vividly red and tacky. As far as chilli heat goes, it's fairly mild and quite sweet. It's used to flavour soups and stews, added to dressings and also makes a mean coating for crisp fried chicken, affectionately coined KFC (Korean fried chicken).

DOENJANG

Literally meaning 'thick paste' in Korean, rich brown doenjang is fermented soya beans without the chilli and is often sold in a coarser-textured form than gochujang, though it's just as sticky. It has a slightly yeasty, nutty aroma to it and a deep savoury edge, and is normally mixed with other pastes to make a dip, or dissolved into stews.

CHILLI BEAN PASTE

Called doubanjiang, this paste is the basis of many Sichuanese dishes, and is very spicy. It has a looser, rougher texture than its Korean counterpart, and does not have the latter's sweetness. It is sometimes made with broad beans as well as soya beans.

YELLOW BEAN PASTE

Contrary to its name, this is a smooth, dark brown sauce, salty and slightly sweet in flavour, used in Chinese cookery, most commonly in noodle and stir-fried dishes.

FERMENTED BLACK BEANS

You can buy salted, fermented black beans whole, usually with ginger, or already ground up and mashed into a sauce. I prefer the whole beans, as they last forever in the cupboard and you can be more versatile with them – some dishes don't require them to be pulverized into a paste. Again, these are made by fermenting and salting black soya beans. They're incredibly salty, so it's best to give them a bit of a rinse before you use them to get rid of the excess salt and to plump them up a bit. Black beans are used as a flavouring: add them to stir-fried vegetables and meat, mash them with some water to make a sauce or scatter a few over fish before you steam it.

HOI SIN SAUCE

Known as the barbecue sauce of the Chinese world, hoi sin is sweet and ubiquitous, and slightly trashy due to its misattribution as plum sauce for roast duck and pancakes (though I find it works perfectly well with it). It's dark to almost black, sticky, thick and, you've guessed it, made with soya beans. It also contains sesame, garlic, salt, vinegar and sometimes chilli to flavour it.

MISO

The backbone of Japanese cuisine, miso comes in many guises; some varieties are made with fermented rice, others with fermented barley, but most types commercially available in the West are made from soya beans. Miso comes in various grades, from white (shiro), the mildest and sweetest miso, to red (aka), which is saltier and more intense, as well as in various forms depending on the Japanese region of origin. You are unlikely to have much choice other than colour, unless you are in a serious Japanese food shop, so the rule of thumb is that red is much stronger and saltier than white, therefore use it sparingly. Miso can be used to make dressings, soups and sauces; try not to bring it to the boil, as all the health benefits are ruined by excessive heat.

SHRIMP PASTES

There are many different variants of shrimp or prawn paste, ranging from solid blocks and pastes with molasses-like textures to very liquid and runny. Confusingly, they are almost all called shrimp (or prawn) paste.

BELACAN

Otherwise known as shrimp paste, belacan is sold as a dark brown, solid block. It's made with fermented ground shrimps and salt, and is most commonly used in Thai, Malaysian, Laotian, Cambodian, Vietnamese and Filipino cuisines. Essential in many curries and sauces, it's usually cooked before consumption. It smells horrid when you give it a sniff out of the packet (a recurring theme, you may find), but once it's cooked it transforms into a mouth-watering flavour – umami in action.

HAE KO

Also called petis udang, this shrimp paste is thick and gloopy like treacle. It's made with sugar for a sweeter consistency, and is mainly served as a condiment in Malaysian cooking with dishes such as popiah rolls and assam laksa.

FINE SHRIMP SAUCE

Also known as fine prawn paste and called mam tom in Vietnamese, this is smooth with a greyish-purple colour, a very liquid paste and is probably the smelliest of them all. It's mixed with chilli, garlic and lime to make a Vietnamese dipping sauce for seafood, and also for marinating meat.

FISH SAUCE

Fish sauce is integral to a number of Asian cuisines, such as Thai, Cambodian and Vietnamese. Made by fermenting fish with salt, it is used as a seasoning both in cooking, as dressings and as dipping sauces. It too contains that essential fifth flavour of umami. Some can be harsher and more pungent than others, so when using fish sauce, use the quantities given as a guide only and taste as you go along.

SESAME PASTE

Not made with soya beans or fish! Sesame paste comes in two forms: light, which you may be more familiar with as tahini, and a dark, rich brown, which is roasted sesame paste. Both have their uses, but I prefer the latter for a more complex flavour. It's mostly used in salad dressings, or for tossing with noodles.

The glorious thing about many Korean stews is that the method generally consists of 'chop, dump in pot and cook'. Perfect for lazy cooks, like me on a weeknight. Or a weekend. Given the short cooking time for this, it has a surprisingly deep flavour. Be sure to use chicken thighs, as the darker meat is far more flavoursome than the breast meat.

DAK DORITANG

Bring a saucepan of water to the boil and drop the chicken pieces in. Simmer for 2 minutes. Drain and rinse the pan and the chicken thoroughly.

Meanwhile, combine all the sauce ingredients in a bowl, add the chicken and toss well.

Place the chicken and sauce back in the clean pan and bring to a simmer. Stir in the potatoes and onions and simmer with the lid on for 10 minutes. Add the carrots and toss in the sauce well, then re-cover and simmer for a further 20 minutes. If it's looking a little dry, add more water, but this is supposed to be nice and thick.

Remove the lid, stir and add the beans or greenery, then simmer gently for another 15 minutes. Serve over steamed white rice with the sliced spring onions garnishing each dish.

4 large bone-in chicken thighs – get your butcher to chop each into 2 for you, or get your cleaver out

6 new potatoes, sliced in half so that they are bite-sized

2 white onions, each chopped into 6

2 carrots, peeled and roughly chopped

handful of green beans – or any greenery you have, really

4 spring onions, diagonally sliced, to garnish

For the sauce:

2 **tbsp** gochujang (*see page 16*)

3 **tbsp** coarse Korean chilli powder (this is not blow-your-face-off stuff but gives it the red colour, so if you use a different chilli powder be careful with quantities)

5 garlic cloves, very finely chopped

5cm (2in) piece of fresh root ginger, peeled and very finely chopped

3 **tbsp** light soy sauce

1 **tbsp** white sugar

1 **tbsp** Shaoxing rice wine

2 **tbsp** tomato ketchup (yes, really)

4 **tbsp** water

This jjigae (Korean for 'stew') is a staple in Korean home cooking, and is very customizable – you can replace the squid with prawns or beef, and the broccoli with courgette or squash. Great for a veg drawer clear-out.

DOENJANG JJIGAE

200g (7oz) fragrant jasmine rice

250ml (9fl oz) water

7.5cm (3in) square of dried kombu (*see page 188*)

1 tsp sesame oil

4 garlic cloves, very finely chopped

1 small onion, diced

4 tbsp doenjang (*see page 16*)

1 potato, peeled and quartered

100g (3½oz) mooli (daikon), peeled and cut into bite-sized chunks

half a block (150–170g) soft silken tofu (bean curd), drained, patted dry with kitchen paper and cut into cubes

3 stems of Tenderstem broccoli

1 large squid tube or **2** small, cut into bite-sized diamond shapes, skin scored

1 spring onion, thinly sliced diagonally, to garnish

Put the rice in a saucepan, add the water and rub the rice grains with your hands until the water turns milky. Drain the rice water into another saucepan and bring to a simmer with the kombu. Simmer gently for 15 minutes. Add more water to the rice and put the rice on to cook, either in a rice cooker or a saucepan (*see page 11 and 47*).

Heat the sesame oil in a saucepan or dolsot (a traditional Korean stone bowl used for cooking stews and rice dishes – *see page 11*). Add the garlic and onion and fry for 5 minutes until the onion has softened. Remove the kombu from the rice water and add the liquid. Add the doenjang, whisking as you go to remove any lumps. Add the potato and the mooli and simmer gently on a low heat for 30 minutes with the lid on.

Add the tofu and simmer for a further 10 minutes, stirring gently. Place the broccoli in a layer on top of the broth along with the squid, re-place the lid and simmer gently for another 5 minutes. By this point the broccoli will be tender and the squid will have curled. Serve with the cooked rice, garnished with the spring onion.

You can buy ssamjang sauce already prepared (it most commonly comes in a green tub), but since you have already gone to the trouble of buying both gochujang and doenjang, there seems little need for another space invader for the fridge. Use this sauce for crudités, and bo ssam – a famous Korean meal of barbecued meats placed in a lettuce leaf with some rice or kimchi. You can also thin this down with a light flavoured oil to dress strong leaves, like rocket, mizuna or watercress.

SSAMJANG SAUCE

SERVES 4

Mix all the ingredients together in a bowl until well combined.

4 tbsp doenjang (*see page 16*)
1½ tbsp gochujang (*see page 16*)
1 spring onion, very finely chopped
1 garlic clove, very finely chopped
3 shallots, very finely chopped
2 tsp clear honey
2 tsp sesame oil
2 tsp white sesame seeds, toasted

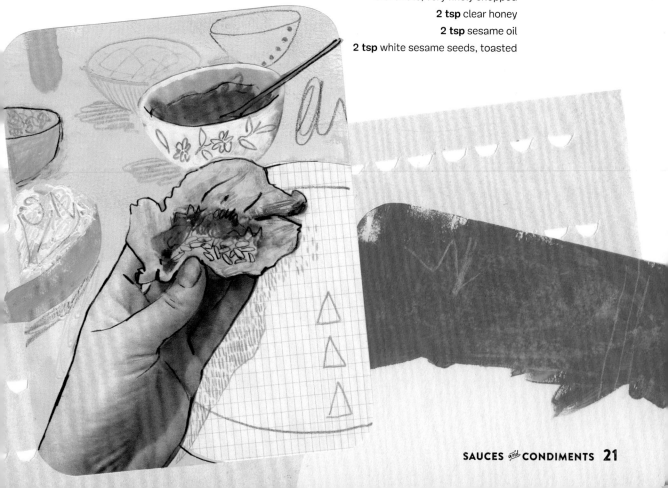

This dish has of course nothing to do with Bolognese as you or I know it. There are no tomatoes or red wine anywhere near this, and in fact the only similarities are that it is made by simmering meat in a sauce and then dressing noodles with it. But I'm still going with the name Chinese Spag Bol. The yellow bean sauce is the base of the dish, and the longer the meat simmers in it, the more flavoursome it becomes. The addition of fresh, crunchy vegetables mixed in at the end makes it feel deceptively light. You've been warned.

 SERVES 4

CHINESE SPAG BOL

2 free-range eggs

2 tbsp cooking oil

2 spring onions, white parts finely chopped, green parts sliced into rings

5 garlic cloves, very finely chopped

2 tsp peeled and very finely chopped fresh root ginger

400g (14oz) fatty minced pork

3 tbsp yellow bean paste (see page 16)

1 tsp light soy sauce

1 tsp dark soy sauce

1 tbsp hoi sin sauce

100ml (3½fl oz) water

2 tbsp Shaoxing rice wine

1 carrot, peeled

½ cucumber

300g (10½oz) fresh Shanghai noodles

Firstly, beat the eggs. Heat 1 tablespoon of the cooking oil in a wok, or nonstick frying pan, until shimmering, add the beaten eggs and cook them over a medium heat until set to make a thin omelette. Remove to a plate and set to one side.

Heat up the rest of the oil in the wok over a medium heat, add the spring onion whites, garlic and ginger and stir-fry until fragrant. Then add the minced pork, breaking up any clumps with your hands, and cook until browned. Add the yellow bean paste, soy sauces and hoi sin sauce with the water and Shaoxing rice wine and simmer for 30 minutes, stirring occasionally. If it's looking a little dry, add a touch more water.

Meanwhile, julienne the carrot and cucumber and set aside. Roll the omelette up and slice finely.

Cook the noodles in a large saucepan of boiling water for a minute, then drain and place in a big serving bowl. Pour the meat sauce on top, then add the vegetables and omelette and stir to combine. Garnish with the greens of the spring onion and serve.

I'm sure that as you read this recipe you'll think 'God, what a lot of faff', and perhaps it is, but it's also incredibly delicious. It combines the best flavours you can get with chilli bean paste – spicy, sour, a little sweet. A whole fish is a real centrepiece, but you can also use fillets, though you lose the most delicious morsel that you, as Chief Cook, get first dibs on – that nugget of cheek, just below the eye.

DEEP-FRIED WHOLE FISH IN CHILLI BEAN SAUCE

SERVES 2–4 WITH OTHER DISHES

1 whole sea bream, rainbow trout or red snapper (about 875g / 1¾lb), gutted and scaled

1 tbsp Shaoxing rice wine

4 garlic cloves

5cm (2in) piece of fresh root ginger, peeled

1 spring onion

100ml (3½fl oz) cooking oil

cornflour, for dusting

2–3 tbsp chilli bean paste (see page 16), depending on how salty your chilli bean paste is – I usually go for 3

2 tsp caster sugar

150ml (5fl oz/¼ pint) water

2 tsp Chinkiang black vinegar

1 tsp potato starch, mixed with **1 tbsp** cold water

Cut 3 slits into the flesh of the fish at a right-angle to the spine, on both sides. Splash with the rice wine, turn over and leave to sit while you work on the sauce ingredients.

Chop the garlic and ginger very finely together. Slice the spring onion into rounds and set aside for garnish.

Heat the oil in a wok until a breadcrumb dropped into it sizzles immediately. Pat the fish dry and coat with cornflour, dusting off the excess. Fry on one side for 5 minutes, then use a fish slice and a metal spatula to carefully turn it over. The cornflour should have prevented the skin from sticking. Fry for a further 4 minutes. You may need to tilt the wok or spoon the oil over the head and tail if the fish is particularly long. Remove carefully and place on a plate lined with kitchen paper.

Drain the oil into a heatproof container, wipe out any cornflour residue from the wok, then pour 2 tablespoons of the oil back into the wok. Fry the chilli bean paste over a medium heat until it is fragrant, then add the garlic and ginger and stir-fry for 2 minutes. Add the sugar and the water, and stir to combine. Carefully put the fish into the wok and braise gently for 5 minutes, spooning the sauce over the fish where it doesn't reach.

By now your fish should be cooked, unless it's really large, in which case put the lid on for a few more minutes until it has cooked – test by poking with a chopstick near the spine; if it's cooked, the flesh will come away easily. Remove the fish to a serving platter. Add the vinegar to the sauce – this is done last to preserve the flavour. Stir the potato starch solution into the wok and simmer until it has thickened, then take off the heat. Spoon the sauce over and around the fish, and garnish with the spring onion rounds.

This is probably one of the most classic and ubiquitous Cantonese dishes, and when done well, black bean sauce is salty and earthy with a funk of the beans' fermented-ness about it. You can use a whole pepper of the one colour, but I like the slight bitterness of the green pepper. You can also substitute chicken or pork for the beef. The bicarbonate of soda marinade is a little restaurant trick to tenderize the meat.

SERVES 4 WITH OTHER DISHES

BEEF IN BLACK BEAN SAUCE

300g (10½oz) rump steak

2 tbsp oyster sauce

1 tbsp cornflour

½ tsp bicarbonate of soda

4 tbsp cooking oil

3 garlic cloves, very finely chopped

2.5cm (1in) piece of fresh root ginger, peeled and finely chopped

3 tbsp fermented black beans (*see page 16*), rinsed well and then drained, chopped and mashed with the back of a spoon

1 large red chilli, sliced into rounds

½ red pepper, cored, deseeded and chopped into bite-sized pieces

½ green pepper, cored, deseeded and chopped into bite-sized pieces

2 tbsp Shaoxing rice wine

1 tsp dark soy sauce

1 tsp sugar

2 spring onions, white parts sliced in half lengthways, green parts sliced into rings

50ml (2fl oz) stock or water

Slice the beef into thin strips against the grain. Mix the oyster sauce, cornflour and bicarbonate of soda together in a bowl, add the beef strips and toss to coat, then cover the bowl with clingfilm and leave to marinate for at least 20 minutes while you prepare the rest of the ingredients.

Add the cooking oil to a wok and heat over a high heat until just below smoking. Add the beef and stir-fry briskly, separating the strips out, for 1 minute until browned. It will sizzle a lot, so be careful. Remove to a plate and set aside.

Drain all but 1 tablespoon of the oil from the wok. Add the garlic and ginger and stir-fry until fragrant. Add the black beans and chilli and carry on stir-frying. Add the peppers, rice wine, soy sauce, sugar, the whites of the spring onions and the stock or water and cook, stirring, for about 5 minutes until the peppers are almost tender.

Return the beef to the wok and stir-fry for a minute more. At this point the sauce should be thickening a little and becoming glossy. Take off the heat and garnish with the spring onion greens.

This Japanese salad is traditionally made with just sesame seeds, but I've upped the flavour factor with three helpings of sesame. The rich, dark brown sesame paste gives it a helping hand to make it creamy and filling, and not at all like the cold vegetable side that it is. Serve it alongside Chicken Katsu Curry (*see page 194*) or other hearty meat dishes.

JAPANESE SPINACH and CUCUMBER SALAD

SERVES

2

AS A SIDE DISH

If using fresh spinach, bring a saucepan of water to the boil. Have a large bowl of cold water with ice cubes nearby. Chop the stems off the spinach and add them to the boiling water, followed by the leaves 10 seconds later. Take off the heat immediately, drain and plunge the leaves and stems into the iced water.

Meanwhile, slice the cucumber into thick matchstick shapes. Put the dark sesame paste, soy sauce, rice vinegar and sesame oil into a clean jar, screw on the lid and shake to mix, or mix together in a bowl. You may need a tablespoon of water to loosen it – it should be the texture of a thick salad dressing, like a Caesar.

Drain the blanched spinach and squeeze dry in a tea towel; likewise if using frozen. Using your fingers, combine with the cucumber, then combine with the dressing, mixing well so that it is all coated.

Pile on to a serving dish and garnish with the toasted sesame seeds.

300g (10½oz) fresh spinach leaves, rinsed well, or frozen whole leaf spinach, defrosted in hot water, drained and squeezed dry

1 cucumber, peeled and deseeded

2 tbsp dark sesame paste (*see page 17*)

1 tbsp light soy sauce

1 tsp rice vinegar

1 tbsp sesame oil

1 tbsp white sesame seeds, toasted

Let's get one thing straight. Shrimp sauce absolutely stinks. It smells like a thousand rotten prawns, mulched into a jar. It is (probably) that. If you open the jar and take a sniff, your head will jerk back, brow furrowed, as if you've been slapped. Something strange happens when you cook with it, though; it changes aroma, and becomes mouthwatering. It smells of the seaside, with added toastiness. It becomes appetizing. If there's any way to get you on board with this death-paste, it's fried chicken. I don't know anyone who doesn't like fried chicken. Juicy meat and a crunchy, flavoursome exterior are key criteria for success.

CHINESE FRIED CHICKEN

SERVES
8
AS A
SNACK

1kg (2lb 4oz) mixture of chicken thighs and wings
3 tbsp fine shrimp sauce (*see page 17*)
2 tsp sugar
2 garlic cloves, mashed
2 tsp ginger juice (grate fresh root ginger and squeeze the pulp to release the juice)
2 tbsp Shaoxing rice wine
2 tbsp oyster sauce
85g (3oz) potato starch
700ml (1¼ pints) cooking oil

Chop the chicken thighs in half through the bone with a cleaver and place in a bowl. Joint the chicken wings by separating the upper wing from the lower wing and wing tip. Add to the bowl.

Mix together the shrimp sauce, sugar, garlic, ginger juice, Shaoxing wine and oyster sauce, then use it to coat the chicken, mixing well. Cover and leave to marinate in the fridge for at least 6 hours, or overnight.

Ten minutes before cooking, add the potato starch to the chicken and mix well.

Heat the oil in a wok or saucepan to 180°C (350°F). Fry the chicken pieces, in batches, for 8–10 minutes until crisp and browned, turning once. Remove and place on a rack to drain.

Serve with **CHILLI & GINGER SAUCE** (*see page 64*) for dipping or sriracha (*see page 109 for homemade, or use shop-bought*).

We've already ascertained the incredible honkiness of shrimp sauce, so with that in mind, I will ask you to open all your windows, turn the extraction on and apologize to anyone in the vicinity, for stinkiness is no reason to turn down something delicious. In this recipe, the tender squid turns a greyish hue, and the celery is essential in bringing a little vibrancy to the dish.

STIR-FRIED SQUID *with* CELERY IN SHRIMP SAUCE

SERVES

2

WITH OTHER DISHES

175g (6oz) squid, cleaned
2 celery sticks
2.5cm (1in) piece of fresh root ginger
3 garlic cloves
1 red chilli
1 spring onion
2 tbsp cooking oil
2 tbsp water
1 tbsp Shaoxing rice wine
1 tsp fine shrimp sauce (*see page 17*)
1 tsp sugar

Cut the squid into largish pieces, as they will curl up when they cook. Using a sharp knife, score the flesh on one side in a crisscross pattern, but not so deep as to cut all the way through.

Top and tail the celery, give it a good wash, then use a vegetable peeler to peel off the outer stringy bits. Slice in half and cut each half lengthways into quarters, then slice into 4cm (1½in) batons.

Scrape the skin off the ginger and very finely chop it with the garlic. Chop the chilli roughly, removing the seeds if you prefer a milder dish. Slice the spring onion diagonally.

Add the oil to a wok over a high heat and heat until just below smoking. Add the ginger, garlic, chilli and celery and stir-fry briskly for 1 minute. Add the water, then stir-fry until it evaporates. Add the squid, rice wine, shrimp sauce and sugar all at once, then stir-fry for 3–4 minutes, constantly moving everything around the pan, until the squid is cooked. Take off the heat, toss the spring onion through and serve immediately.

For a dish with so few ingredients, this is insanely delicious. It might be in part something to do with the fatty richness of pork belly, or the basic human love of sugar or the savoury bomb of fish sauce, but combined it is a beautiful thing. I particularly love the gelatinous quality of the skin when it is slowly braised, though some get squeamish about it. Roll your eyes at them until they at least try a bit, and then rejoice when they see the light.

CARAMEL PORK BELLY

Add the oil to a small frying pan on a medium heat and brown the pork cubes on all sides. It doesn't need to be cooked through at this stage. Remove from the pan and drain on kitchen paper.

In a saucepan big enough to just hold the pork, heat the sugar over a low heat until it has dissolved and caramelized to a deep golden colour, swirling the pan once it has started to melt but resisting the temptation to stir.

Take off the heat and stir in 50ml (2fl oz) of warm water, being careful to stay clear of the spluttering burning hot caramel – if the sugar should seize into a hard state, bring to the boil to return the caramel to a liquid form.

Stir the pork into the caramel, then stir in the fish sauce with another 3 tablespoons of water. Cover and cook very gently for about an hour until the meat is tender, turning the pork cubes halfway through the cooking time. Add the ground pepper, put the lid back on and cook for a further 5 minutes.

Serve with plain rice and steamed vegetables (*see page 84*), or the **SMACKED CUCUMBER SALAD** below.

1 tsp cooking oil

450g (1lb) pork belly slices with skin, cut into bite-sized cubes

3 tbsp sugar

2½ tbsp fish sauce

½ tsp ground black pepper

SERVES 2 AS A SIDE

1 large cucumber

2 tsp salt

2½ tbsp rice vinegar

3 garlic cloves, very finely chopped

2 tsp palm sugar

2 tsp chilli oil

2 tsp toasted sesame oil

1 tsp light soy sauce

SMACKED CUCUMBER SALAD

Lay the cucumber on a chopping board and smack lightly with a cleaver or a rolling pin. Chop roughly and add to a colander, sprinkling with the salt. Leave for 30 minutes, then rinse and pat dry with kitchen paper.

Mix together the vinegar, garlic, sugar, chilli oil, sesame oil and soy sauce in a bowl. Add the cucumber to the mix and leave to soak up the flavours for 10 minutes before serving.

Nuoc cham is a Vietnamese dipping sauce, commonly served with noodle salads, spring rolls, summer rolls and banh xeo, a crêpe-like pancake stuffed with bean sprouts and protein. Essentially, this sauce should be made with the component parts as you prefer. So keep tasting and adding them according to your taste, as you might prefer it more sour, more sweet, or more or less spicy. This is how I like mine.

GRILLED AUBERGINES *with* NUOC CHAM

SERVES 2 WITH OTHER DISHES

Slice the Asian aubergines (if using) lengthways into quarters, keeping the stem intact so that it holds the aubergine together. Heat the oil in a wok until almost smoking, then turn the heat down to medium and fry the aubergines well, turning occasionally. Do not burn. Transfer the aubergines to an ovenproof dish. Cook under a preheated medium grill for 20 minutes, turning the aubergines halfway through.

Chop the mint finely, and the coriander leaves roughly. Set aside. If you have roots on your coriander stalks, wash them well, chop them finely and add them to the mortar to be ground into the nuoc cham sauce.

To assemble, place the aubergines in a serving dish while warm, top with the mint and coriander and dress with the nuoc cham. Finally, scatter over the cashews.

3 Asian aubergines, or use **1** European aubergine, cut into fingers
4 tbsp vegetable oil
½ handful of mint
handful of fresh coriander
1 quantity Nuoc Cham (*see below*)
handful of toasted cashews, roughly crushed

SERVES 2

NUOC CHAM

1 fat garlic clove
2 tsp soft dark brown sugar
1 red bird's eye chilli (use more if you like it really hot, less if you don't)
juice of 1 lime
2 tbsp fish sauce, or to taste
2 tbsp water, or to taste

Peel the garlic clove and crush with the sugar using a pestle and mortar until it is a smooth paste. Deseed the chilli and chop it roughly, then add to the mortar and give it a good pestling. Add the lime juice and mix well. Add 1 tablespoon of the fish sauce and taste. Add 1 tablespoon water and taste. Keep doing this until you have the desired piquancy or pungency that you like. Remember, you can always add but you can't take away.

Hoi sin sauce has that heady, fruity sweetness that goes perfectly with pork, and becomes beautifully sticky when roasted or grilled. This is a ridiculously simple recipe with maximum flavour results; all you have to do is make sure your ribs are nice and fatty.

HOI SIN & GINGER PORK RIBS

Put the ribs into a large dish. Whizz all the sauce ingredients in a blender until you have a smooth consistency. Smear all over the ribs, using your hands to make sure they are all covered. Cover the dish with clingfilm and leave to marinate in the fridge overnight.

Preheat the oven to 200°C (400°F) Gas Mark 6. Line a roasting tray with foil and set a rack over it. Pour boiling water into the tray, lift the ribs out of the marinade, reserving what's left, and place the ribs on the rack, bone side down. Roast for 30 minutes, then turn the oven down to 160°C (325°F) Gas Mark 3, add more water if it's looking a little dry and roast for a further hour.

Simmer the remaining marinade in a small saucepan for 3 minutes. Chop the ribs up into portions along the length of the bones and drizzle the sauce on top.

Serve with **CLOUD EAR FUNGUS & TOFU BAMBOO SALAD** (*see page 207*).

1.5kg (3lb 5oz) rack of pork ribs

For the sauce:
1 onion, roughly chopped
8 garlic cloves, peeled
15cm (6in) piece of fresh root ginger, peeled
160ml (5½fl oz) hoi sin sauce
4 tbsp orange juice
2 tbsp sesame oil
2 tbsp Shaoxing rice wine
2 tbsp light soy sauce
1 tbsp dark soy sauce
1 tbsp tomato purée
1 tsp sherry vinegar
1 tsp black peppercorns

In Malaysian, Singaporean and Indonesian cookery, 'sambal' refers to a sauce, paste or dip that includes chillies, be they cooked or fresh. There are many different kinds of sambal, and the recipe opposite is categorized by the addition of shrimp paste that is 'tumis', which means stir-fried – the chillies and shrimp paste are cooked together with oil to make a rich and fragrant sauce. But you can experiment with other ingredients using a base of chillies; combine them with tamarind purée to make a tart sambal assam, or add tomatoes for a milder, sweeter sambal. Try it with fried dried anchovies, or add raw chillies, tomatoes and lime juice – almost like a Mexican salsa. Sambal oelek is the raw chilli paste version. This is a great dish for guests. The mackerel is stuffed to the brim with sambal and is perfect for people to pick at. Although traditionally it is deep-fried, I prefer to oil the skin and grill it, as it's far easier and you still get to enjoy crisp fish skin. Serve with bright stir-fried greens, some noodles and steamed rice.

STUFFED SAMBAL MACKEREL

Turn your grill on to the highest setting to heat up. Line up your mackerel with the head facing you and cut 2 slits down either side of the backbone of the fish. Use a teaspoon to stuff the slits with the sambal belacan. If you have any left over, this can be smeared into the cavity too.

Line a roasting tray with foil and set a rack over it. Oil both sides of the mackerel with your hands and place the fish on the rack so that it is standing up – you may have to prop it up with balled foil. Grill for 5 minutes with the mackerel at least 18cm (7in) away from the heating element – keep an eye on it, as you don't want it to burn.

Remove the props so that the mackerel lies carefully on its side and grill for another 5 minutes, then turn it over and do the same. By now the mackerel should be cooked; the flesh in the middle should pull away easily if so, but for mackerel on the large side, increase the cooking time to 8–10 minutes per side and turn the heat down a little so that it doesn't burn.

Place the fish on a serving dish, squeeze the lime over it and drizzle with the soy sauce to serve.

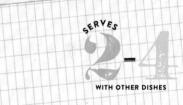

SERVES

2–4

WITH OTHER DISHES

1 large or **2 small** whole mackerel, gutted

1 quantity Sambal Belacan (*see opposite*)

1 tbsp cooking oil, for oiling

1 lime, halved, for squeezing

1 tbsp light soy sauce

SAMBAL BELACAN

MAKES
1 SMALL JAR

Snip the soaked chillies in half and discard the seeds. Bash together using a pestle and mortar, together with the fresh red chillies, shallots, garlic and lemon grass, adding 1 tablespoon of the cooking oil to help it along, although as the mixture should be quite fine, a small blender, if you have one, is much easier.

Toast the shrimp paste in a dry wok or frying pan – it will be… aromatic – then add to the mix and blend or pound again until it is incorporated.

Heat up the remaining 2 tablespoons of oil in a wok over a medium heat and add the lot. Cook on a medium heat, stirring it often, for 8 or so minutes until it has darkened (but not burned!) to a rich brown colour. Stir in the palm sugar and tamarind purée, simmer for another minute, then take off the heat. Scoop into a bowl to cool.

You can transfer this to a sterilized jar and cover with vegetable oil, then keep in the fridge for up to a week.

5 long thin dried red chillies, soaked in just-boiled water for 20 minutes, then drained

2 large fresh red chillies, deseeded and roughly chopped

5 shallots, thinly sliced

3 garlic cloves, very finely chopped

1 lemon grass stalk, woody outer layers removed

3 tbsp cooking oil

½ tbsp belacan (shrimp paste) (*see page 17*)

1 tbsp palm sugar

½ tbsp tamarind purée

I've mentioned before that belacan (shrimp paste) becomes much more palatable and less smelly once you cook it, and this dish proves it so, even with the gentlest of cooking. The pure, unflavoured rice takes on the shrimp paste flavour, and if you're someone that likes a little variation in each mouthful, you'll probably enjoy the colourful bits and pieces lining the plate, allowing you to customize each mouthful.

SERVES 2

THAI SHRIMP PASTE RICE

175g (6oz) boneless pork shoulder, sliced into thin strips

3 tbsp palm sugar

3 tbsp water

1½ tbsp light soy sauce

2 tsp dark soy sauce

200g (7oz) fragrant jasmine rice

3 tbsp cooking oil

2 free-range eggs, beaten with a splash of fish sauce

2 tbsp dried shrimps, washed

1 Granny Smith apple or green mango

1 tbsp belacan (shrimp paste) (see page 17), mashed with 1 tbsp water

100g (3½oz) green beans, blanched and diced

7 red shallots, thinly sliced

100g (3½oz) cucumber, peeled and diced

2 lime wedges

For the sauce:

3 red bird's eye chillies

4 tbsp rice vinegar

1 tbsp water

Add the pork, palm sugar, water and dark and light soy sauces to a small saucepan. Simmer over a medium heat with the lid off for 30–40 minutes, stirring often, until the mixture has reduced in liquid and is dark and sticky. Add a splash or two more of water if needed.

Set the rice to cook in a rice cooker or saucepan (see page 47). Meanwhile, swirl 1 tablespoon of the cooking oil around a wok on a medium heat. Pour the beaten eggs into the wok and allow to set, flipping once. Remove the omelette from the wok, roll and slice thinly.

Chop the chillies for the sauce up roughly and add to the vinegar, along with the water. Leave to marinate.

Wipe the wok out and heat up another tablespoon of cooking oil until just below smoking. Pat the dried shrimps dry and add to the oil, stir-frying for 30 seconds–1 minute. Set to one side.

At this point, julienne the apple or peel and stone the green mango ready to serve so that it doesn't go brown from hanging around too long.

By this stage, the rice should have cooked. Mix the shrimp paste into the rice, turning the rice over and over gently to mix in the paste evenly. It may take about 10 minutes, but you'll be left with brown-speckled rice.

To serve, lightly oil a rice bowl with the some of the remaining tablespoon of oil and pack half the rice into the bowl, then turn out on a plate. Repeat with the other portion. Around the edge of each plate, arrange half the green beans, shallots, omelette, cucumber, fried shrimps and the apple or mango. Spoon a little of the sweet pork on top of the fried rice, and balance a wedge of lime on top. Serve with the chilli vinegar sauce.

For me, miso is comforting, as well as soothing, and no more so than when it is coating a chunk of slow-cooked, wibbly pork belly. The Japanese believe miso has health-giving properties – how better to treat such an ingredient than to flavour pork fat with it?

MISO-BRAISED PORK BELLY

Cut the pork belly into large cubes. Place in a saucepan of boiling water and boil for a couple of minutes; this is so that any scum comes floating to the surface now, and not in your stew.

Drain, rinse and set the saucepan back on the heat. Put the oil and the onion in a layer on the base. You don't want them cooking much at the moment. Add the pork belly in a layer on top. Pour over the sake, then the water. Cut a piece of nonstick baking paper so that it fits into the pot nicely, then place the lid on. Cook on the lowest heat (you want a bare simmer) for 1½ hours.

Add the mirin, soy sauce and sugar as well as the mooli, re-cover and cook for another hour. By now, the pork belly and the mooli should be tender; if not, cook a little longer. Discard the paper, then take out a ladleful of the stock, mix into the white and red miso until it dissolves, then add to the stew. Cook on the barest simmer for a further 15 minutes – don't let it boil, as it will ruin any nutritional benefit in the miso.

Slice the white parts of the spring onions and add to the stew. Julienne the green parts of the spring onions and set aside for the garnish.

This isn't a thick stew, as much of the liquid won't have evaporated, so best to serve it in a large bowl or a pasta dish. Serve over white rice, garnished with the spring onion greens.

SERVES 4 GREEDY PEOPLE OR 6 WITH OTHER DISHES

700g (1lb 9oz) boneless pork belly, skin on or off – if yours comes with ribs, simply remove them and use them for another dish, or for stock or congee (*see page 58*)

1 tbsp cooking oil

1 white onion, finely sliced

190ml (6½fl oz) sake

700ml (1¼ pints) water

1 tbsp mirin

1½ tbsp light soy sauce

2 tsp sugar

450g (1lb) mooli (daikon), peeled and sliced into rounds about 2.5cm (1in) thick

3 tbsp white miso (*see page 16*)

2 tsp red miso (*see page 16*)

2 spring onions

Although miso is a traditional Japanese ingredient, it also works well in sauces and butters. Its salty-sweetness can be a little too strong for it to be used entirely on its own, but when combined with fats (in this case, mayonnaise and butter), it makes it not only easily spreadable, but also has a more balanced flavour. You can make the Miso Mayo below from scratch, or alternatively stir miso paste into ready-made mayonnaise, tasting as you go for the desired strength of flavour.

SEARED SALMON & MISO MAYO SANDWICH

SERVES 4

Pat the salmon dry, then dust with the chilli powder and a little salt.

Add the oil and the salmon fillets, skin side down, to a cold nonstick frying pan. This encourages the skin to crisp. Turn the heat on to medium and cook the salmon fillets until the skin has crisped, around 4–6 minutes. Turn over and cook for a further minute, depending on the thickness of your fillets.

Split your rolls and toast the inside. Smear with plenty of the miso mayo on both sides. Lay watercress on the bottom, along with the mooli, slightly overlapping in a fan shape. Place the salmon fillet on top, skin-side up, then top with the other half of the roll. Slice in half to serve.

2 salmon fillets, skin on – tail end is better, as they are flatter
chilli powder, for dusting
salt
1 tbsp cooking oil
2 ciabatta rolls
1 quantity Miso Mayo (*see below*)
handful of watercress, chopped
Pickled Mooli (*see page 157*)

MISO MAYO

MAKES ENOUGH FOR 2 SANDWICHES

pinch of salt
2 free-range egg yolks
400ml (14fl oz) groundnut oil
juice of ½ lemon
2½ tbsp white miso (*see page 16*)
1 tsp Dijon mustard

Make sure the egg yolks, miso and oil are at room temperature before starting.

Add the salt to the egg yolks in a bowl and beat well with a hand or electric whisk. Add about half the oil in drops at first, making sure that each drop is incorporated, graduating to a very fine stream while beating the egg yolk mixture vigorously. I find it's far easier to rope in an unsuspecting housemate or partner to do the whisking while you do the pouring. When the mixture becomes thick and a little lumpy, add the lemon juice, whisking well. Once you've added half the oil, whisk in 1 tablespoon of the miso and the mustard. Carry on whisking in the oil in a slow stream until you have your desired consistency. Add the remaining miso and mix well to combine. If it becomes too thick, let it down with a little water, bit by bit. Keep in a sterilized jar in the fridge for up to 3 days.

1 tbsp red miso (*see page 16*)

20g (¾oz) butter, soft but not liquid

2 corn on the cob, freshly cooked
(*see introduction*)

MISO-BUTTERED CORN ON THE COB

SERVES

2

There are several ways of cooking corn on the cob. If you've got the weather for a barbecue, then there is no better method than cooking the cobs in their husks over indirect heat (though soak them in water first). At other times, cobs simmered in salted water aren't a bad alternative.

Using a spoon, combine the miso with the butter in a bowl until it is well incorporated. Slather your just-cooked corn with it.

➡OTHER IDEAS

You can add what you like to the base butter recipe; a little garlic grated into the butter mix, or shiso leaves finely chopped work nicely. I also like a little citrus, such as grated lemon or lime rind in the base butter with the juice squeezed over the cob. You can use the butter to flavour other vegetables too, such as steamed broccoli or grilled asparagus, and it also works well on top of cooked meat, such as steak, or fish. Add sesame seeds and a little vinegar, and replace the butter with groundnut or olive oil for a salad dressing. What it definitely doesn't need is salt.

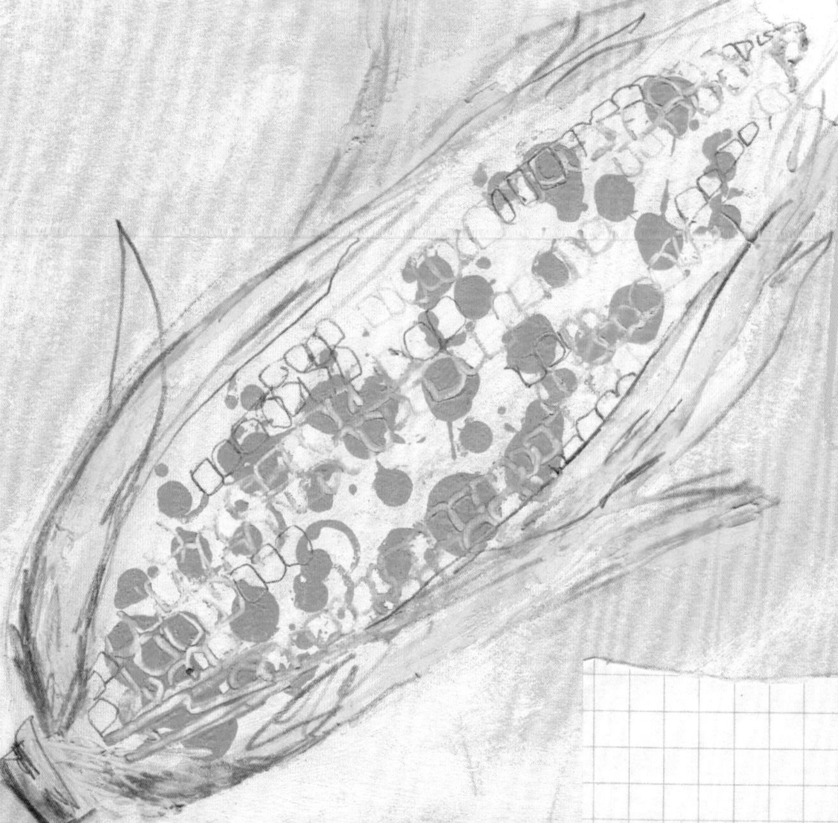

CHAPTER

RICE &NOO DLES

RICE & NOODLES

Ask any Asian what one food they couldn't live without, and they might well say rice. If you held a gun to my head, I would probably say the same – I can't imagine life without those pearly white grains, steamed until fluffy, ready to receive any sauce you throw at them. The backbone of many an Asian meal, rice is a bland foil for the spread of dishes that a typical dinner will have, a necessity to loosen the flavours. It's associated with one of my earliest food memories – as a child, I trotted off to the rice cooker for a second helping and was sternly told off for not helping my elders to it first.

It is also a comfort; when I'm unwell, rice cooked for hours into a rice porridge called congee is life-giving. When I'm feeling lazy, a load of ingredients chucked in the rice cooker along with the rice all cook happily together into a one-pot meal. When my palate is jaded or I just can't be bothered, a spoonful of tomato ketchup stirred into a steaming bowl while sat in front of the TV does the trick; a stuck childhood memory of my best friend's Thai mother and her favourite snack.

Noodles, though. Where rice is the comfortable norm, noodles are the sexy little number. Egg noodles, rice noodles, bean thread noodles, mung bean noodles, sweet potato noodles, wheat noodles, fresh noodles, dried noodles… the possibilities stretch before you endlessly. Much like pasta shapes, some noodles suit certain sauces better than others. Some have a texture that need a lighter dressing, some can hold their own against heavy, rich sauces, while others are made to bathe or to be dunked into soups. Some simply look nicer in their appropriate preparation.

This chapter attempts to showcase the very best of rice and noodles in the sorts of dishes they're best suited to. This is by no means an exhaustive list (that could go on for reams), but rather the types most readily available to the Western consumer.

RICE

If you cook Asian food a lot, you really must buy a rice cooker. They are inexpensive, they cook rice perfectly and keep it warm and it's one less pan on the hob. Alternatively, you can cook rice in a saucepan with a tight-fitting lid (*see opposite*). Never salt the rice; the dishes that go with it are seasoned enough.

(1) GLUTINOUS (STICKY) RICE

Glutinous rice is a type of rice that becomes very sticky when cooked. The glutinous aspect doesn't pertain to gluten, but rather the way in which the rice behaves – when steamed, it becomes very dense and you can pick up a whole clump in one go. It's often used in dim sum; the Cantonese wrap it in lotus leaves with flavourings like chicken and salted egg, before it is steamed. Always soak this rice overnight to reduce cooking time and improve texture. It's best steamed using the splatter guard and saucepan method (see below), or steamed within something.

(2) BLACK GLUTINOUS (STICKY) RICE

This is prepared in the same way as the white variety but more often used for sweet rather than savoury dishes.

(3) SHORT-GRAIN RICE

Although less sticky than its glutinous cousin, short-grain rice is still sticky enough to hold together. It is used seasoned with vinegar for sushi and commonly eaten with Japanese and Korean meals.

(4) LONG-GRAIN RICE

This includes fragrant jasmine and basmati rice, which has a distinct flavour and texture that I associate more with Indian food. Brown rice is being eaten more and more nowadays, and you can opt for that if you like, but it doesn't have quite the sauce-mopping qualities that white rice does.

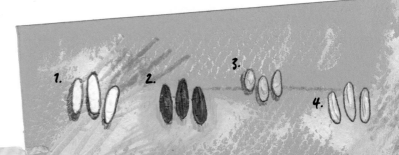

COOKING RICE WITHOUT A RICE COOKER

Rinse the grains well. Working to the ratio of 225g (8oz) uncooked rice for 2 people, cook in 290ml (10fl oz) boiling water in a saucepan with a tight-fitting lid. Once the water boils, reduce the heat to low, place the lid on top and simmer for 10–12 minutes. Once done, remove from the heat, fluff the grains up with a fork and replace the lid to steam for a further 10 minutes.

STEAMING GLUTINOUS (STICKY) RICE

Traditionally, the Thais cook glutinous rice using a large bamboo steamer. These are big contraptions and allow the rice to cook in steam instead of being submerged in water. Not many of us have the space for this at home, so an easier and far more popular method is to steam the rice using a splatter guard. These are metal discs with a handle that you place over frying pans to stop oil from splattering out. You can buy these inexpensively and in varying sizes; buy one bigger than a frying pan you have that has a deep lip, or a saucepan.

To cook enough rice for two, soak 200g (7oz) of glutinous (sticky) rice in water for 3 hours, then drain. Fill a saucepan or frying pan to halfway with boiling water, place the splatter guard over it and add the rice in a pile in the middle. You should leave about 5cm (2in) of air between the rice and the water. Bring the water to a gentle boil, then place a metal or heatproof plastic (glass or ceramic can be too heavy) mixing bowl over the rice and steam for 30 minutes, turning it over once so that it does not become mushy. If you're cooking for a larger number of people, you may have to spread the rice out more and cook it for longer.

TOASTED GROUND RICE

This is essential for a lot of Thai salads like larb and dips for its nutty flavour and crunch. It also soaks up excess moisture in a dish, and sometimes binds it together. If a recipe calls for it, even just a little, it's always worth adding it for the flavour and texture profile it contributes. Glutinous (sticky) rice grains are best for this, as they break up more easily. To prepare, add the rice to a dry frying pan over a medium-low heat and, just like you might with pine nuts, toast them until they are golden brown but not burned. This will take at least 10 minutes, with regular stirring and shaking. Don't be tempted to use a higher heat, as this will burn the grains.

Next, you can use a spice or coffee grinder or a pestle and mortar to grind the rice up. The former gives a more uniform texture; the latter requires you to put in some elbow grease. Cover the top of the mortar and pestle and use a gentle pound-and-twist technique, otherwise your grains might ping off on to the kitchen floor before long. Grind to a fine powder and use to sprinkle on your dishes. You can keep the leftovers in an airtight container for a couple of weeks, but freshly ground really is best.

RICE NOODLES

A multitude of textures awaits you with noodles, all ready to be made into whatever you want. Rice noodles are defined by their width and shape. My favourite of them all, ho fun, are wide, flat rice noodles most commonly bought fresh from the fridge section of the Asian supermarket. These are slippery and slithery in soups or loose sauces – a ruiner of white clothing – but are also substantial enough to take on the char and smoke of a wok in stir-fried dishes. Char kway teow, almost a national dish of Singapore and Malaysia, uses ho fun, and would be an entirely different and lesser dish without the glistening soft folds of these noodles. Many famous dishes are, in fact, named after the shape of noodle within them.

(1) RICE VERMICELLI
(MEI FUN, BEEHOON OR BUN)

These are the thinnest, most delicate type of noodle. The equivalent of angel hair pasta, they are used for salads and stir-fries. You can use them in noodle soups too. Soak in hot water for 10 minutes, then drain well to use.

(2) KWAY CHAP (RICE FLAKES)

Shaped like Doritos, i.e. big transparent squares or triangles, you soak these in hot water for 10 minutes, drain and add to richly spiced broths, such as in Kway Chap (see page 64). They work equally as well in lighter broths, but also stir-fried. When cooked, they roll within themselves a little, trapping sauce inside, for a more substantial but still slippery and smooth mouthful.

(3) RICE STICKS
(FLAT RICE NOODLES OR PHO)

A wider variety of dried rice noodle, you soak them in boiling water for about 10 minutes until tender, drain them and add them to noodle soups, whereby they become smooth and silky. Or stir-fry them, as in pad Thai.

(4) JIANGXI (GUILIN, THICK RICE VERMICELLI OR BUN)

Confusingly, the Vietnamese call any round rice noodle 'bun', whatever the thickness. Almost as thick as spaghetti, these noodles are used in laksa (a rich, coconutty noodle soup), salads and the famous 'bun' noodle soups of Vietnam (though they're always used fresh in Vietnam – alas, not easy to find elsewhere). They need to be cooked in boiling water for 3–7 minutes, depending on the brand. They have a wonderfully chewy texture.

EGG NOODLES

So-called egg and wheat noodles are slightly confusing because, while some are made with egg, others don't contain egg at all but are still called egg noodles because they look yellow. It's best to check the ingredients.

(5) ROUND EGG NOODLES
(HOKKIEN)

You'll find these noodles in the fridge cabinet, looking like a thicker, more vibrantly yellow spaghetti. Elastic and chewy, these withstand being stir-fried very well and are ideal for rich, thick noodle soups. Refresh in boiling water to remove the excess oil, then proceed.

1.

2.

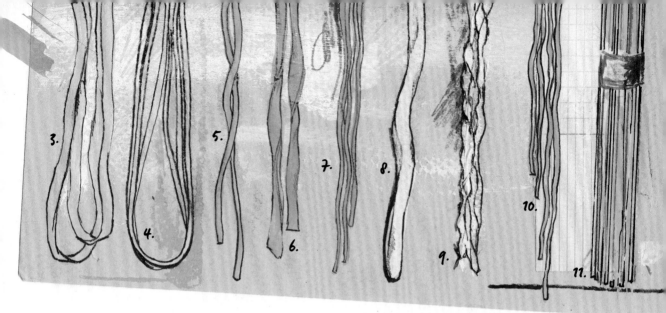

(6) FLAT EGG NOODLES

Sold dried in bundles, these are great tossed with a dressing, cold as a salad or stir-fried. Cook in simmering water for about 4 minutes until the bundle has relaxed, then drain well and toss with a little cooking oil to prevent from sticking before using.

(7) HONG KONG NOODLES
(WONTON NOODLES OR LO MEIN)

Sold fresh in the chiller cabinet, these are often tossed with a dressing (lo means 'mix it up' and mein means 'noodle', so refers to this method of preparation specifically) or used in noodle soups. Refresh in boiling water for 1 minute to remove some of the flour on the surface of the noodles, drain and rinse with cold water, then plunge back into boiling water briefly to warm them before dressing. You can also buy these dried for convenience, and the top-quality versions contain shrimp (prawn) roe – you will see tiny dots of it in each noodle strand. Cook the nests by simmering in boiling water for 3–5 minutes, then drain but keep the water the noodles were cooked in for dipping the noodles into or sipping on the side, as this water is flavoured with the shrimp roe.

(8) SHANGHAI NOODLES & UDON

Shanghai noodles, usually found in the fridge section, are much like udon, which are Japanese wheat noodles. They are sometimes square and sometimes round and thicker than spaghetti, hence people often saying they resemble worms. The most satisfying udon are the frozen or vacuum-packed varieties, but they are also sold dry. Heat through with boiling water until the udon cake has loosened, then drain and dress, add to noodle soups or stir-fry. Whereas udon are eaten both hot in broth and cold with a dipping sauce, Shanghai noodles are usually stir-fried and served hot.

(9 & 10) GLASS NOODLES
(BEAN THREAD OR CELLOPHANE) &
MUNG BEAN SHEET NOODLES

There are two main types of these noodles, made either with mung bean starch (9) or sweet potato starch (10). Both are used in braised dishes, salads, spring rolls and soups, though the sweet potato variety, used more commonly in Korean cooking, is thicker and has a chewier texture. Smooth, slippery and jelly-like, glass noodles are so-named for their see-through quality. Mung bean sheets are noodles made from the same starch but in varying widths, and can sometimes come in sheets for you to break off as you see fit. Soak in hot water for 10–30 minutes, depending on width, before using.

(11) SOBA (BUCKWHEAT) NOODLES

Soba noodles are always thin, and the Japanese eat them hot, cold, in soup or with a dipping sauce. In Korea, they are almost always eaten cold in the summertime. Cook as per the packet instructions, then rinse and refresh in iced water.

E-FU (YI MEIN)

These egg noodles are round and sold deep-fried into flat discs about the size of your palm. They have a spongy texture when cooked, and are often eaten at birthdays for longevity, since the noodles themselves are always long strands, symbolizing long life. These are most commonly eaten in restaurants, with luxury ingredients such as lobster and crab.

RAMEN

Chinese in origin, ramen noodles are now often synonymous with the Japanese noodle soup dish. They are wheat noodles made with alkaline water to give them elasticity and come in thick or thin, wavy or straight varieties, depending on the type of ramen broth they're destined for. Instant noodles, since they mostly come in soup, are often called instant ramen.

Here, I've used glutinous rice, which clumps together once cooked, to stuff a chicken for a kind of alternative Sunday roast, if you will. The rice is flavoured with all the chicken juices and is glistening with fat, compact and rich. You only need a little to accompany your meat.

ROAST RICE-STUFFED CHICKEN

SERVES 4

Bash the whole garlic cloves with the piece of ginger using a pestle and mortar until you have a paste. Add the five-spice, vegetable oil, soy sauces, oyster sauce and fermented bean curd and pound together into a sauce. Rub over your chicken (reserving any left over), cover and leave to marinate in the fridge overnight.

To cook, preheat the oven to 220°C (425°F) Gas Mark 7. Heat the oil in a wok and fry the Chinese sausage on a medium heat until it changes colour a little. Add the garlic and ginger, then mix well. Add the mandarin peel to the wok along with the rice, then stir in the rice wine and soy sauces. Cook for 5 minutes, turning the rice over and over again, until it is fairly dry. Stir in the spring onions, then leave to cool completely.

Using a tablespoon, scoop the cooled rice into the cavity of the chicken, pushing it further down the cavity to make room for more. Stuff until the cavity is full but not bursting. Tip the chicken up and carefully pour the water into the cavity, then place back down in a roasting tray. Roast for 20 minutes, then turn the oven down to 160°C (325°F) Gas Mark 3 and roast for another hour and 10 minutes, basting often. During the last 5 minutes, brush the chicken skin with the honey.

Give the thigh joint a poke for doneness – the juices should run clear. Remove from the oven and leave to rest for 20 minutes before carving. Scoop a little rice out for each portion of chicken and spoon out a little of the juices from the bottom of the roasting dish and drizzle over each serving. Serve with garlicky greens.

3 garlic cloves, peeled
2.5cm (1in) piece of fresh root ginger, peeled
½ tsp five-spice powder (*see page 205 for homemade*)
1 tbsp vegetable oil
1 tbsp dark soy sauce
2 tbsp light soy sauce
3 tbsp oyster sauce
1 cube of red fermented tofu (bean curd) (*see page 163*)
1 whole chicken, about 1.5kg (3lb 5oz)
150ml (5fl oz/¼ pint) water
1 tbsp clear honey

For the rice

1 tbsp cooking oil
2 Chinese sausages, sliced into thin rounds
2 garlic cloves, very finely chopped
1 slice of fresh root ginger, peeled and very finely chopped
1 whole dried mandarin peel, soaked in just-boiled water for 10 minutes until soft and then drained and finely chopped
200g (7oz) glutinous (sticky) rice, soaked in cold water overnight, drained
3 tbsp Shaoxing rice wine
2 tbsp light soy sauce
1 tsp dark soy sauce
3 spring onions, finely chopped

This is the type of thing that Hong Kong's cuisine is famous for.
A little bit Chinese, a little bit Westernized; slightly trashy but
not regarded as so. This baked pork chop rice was a favourite of
mine from Café de Coral in Hong Kong. Open for breakfast, lunch
and dinner, it's a fast food restaurant chain, one my grandmother
took me to frequently – this is pure nostalgia for me. Along with
this recipe is the standard method for egg fried rice that you can
embellish to your heart's content to make a complete meal in itself.

HONG KONG-STYLE
BAKED PORK CHOP RICE

SERVES
2

Firstly, mix the rice wine and soy sauces together in a dish, add the pork
chops and turn to coat. Cover the dish with clingfilm and leave to marinate
in the fridge while you prepare the rest of the ingredients.

For the egg fried rice, pour some boiling water over the peas to defrost them,
then drain. Heat the oil in a wok over a high heat, swirling to coat the sides,
and add the rice, breaking up any clumps with your hands as you go. Leave
the rice to cook over the high heat until you see individual grains jumping –
then they're ready to be stirred. Add the peas and mix with the rice, then
move to one side of the wok. Crack both eggs into the wok and add the soy
sauce. Stir-fry briskly for 30 seconds, then take off the heat and add the
spring onion. Transfer the rice to an ovenproof dish, or 2 individual dishes.

Preheat the oven to 220°C (425°F) Gas Mark 7. Heat the oil for the sauce in
a saucepan, add the onion, garlic and tomatoes and cook over a medium
heat until the tomatoes are starting to break down a little, the onion is
translucent and the garlic is fragrant. Add the ketchup, Worcestershire
sauce, sugar, salt and water, then simmer gently for 10–15 minutes. Mix
the cornflour with a little cold water until smooth, stir into the pan and cook
until thickened, then take off the heat.

While the sauce is simmering, heat the remaining 2 tablespoons of oil in a
nonstick frying pan. Shake off the marinade from the pork chops and dust
with cornflour, then fry in the hot oil over a medium heat for 5 minutes each
side until cooked. Leave to rest for 5 minutes and then slice.

Top the rice with the pork, then pour the sauce evenly over the pork slices.
Scatter the 2 cheeses on top and bake for 15 minutes so that the cheese
has melted and everything is bubbling.

1 tbsp Shaoxing rice wine

1 tbsp light soy sauce

1 tsp dark soy sauce

2 pork chops off the bone, fat scored
(this prevents them from curling up)

2 tbsp cooking oil

cornflour, for dusting

For the egg fried rice:

50g (1¾oz) frozen peas

2 tbsp cooking oil

250g (9oz) cooked (preferably the day
before) and cooled fragrant jasmine rice

2 free-range eggs

1 tsp light soy sauce

1 spring onion, diagonally sliced

For the sauce:

1 tbsp cooking oil

½ white onion, roughly chopped

2 garlic cloves, very finely chopped

3 tomatoes, roughly chopped

6 tbsp tomato ketchup

1 tbsp Worcestershire sauce

1 tsp sugar

pinch of salt

100ml (3½fl oz) water

1 tsp cornflour

handful of grated mozzarella cheese

handful of grated strong Cheddar cheese

My parents used to make me this soup for breakfast once a month or so, whenever we had rice left over from a weekend dinner. It is everything I love in a breakfast; hot, nourishing and with bright and sparky flavours. The condiments are served on the side for you to help yourself, so that every bite and every slurp of soup can be customized – you'll need a few saucers for these. There is, of course, nothing quite like chilli and garlic to wake up to, and these days I find it's a pretty wonderful hangover cure.

THAI RICE SOUP

Add the stock, celery and ginger to a large saucepan. Chop the lemon grass stalk in half and add to the pot with the rice, then bring the stock to a simmer. Mix the minced chicken with the salt and white pepper, roll into small balls and drop carefully into the soup. Simmer on a gentle heat for 15–20 minutes until cooked through.

Meanwhile, chop the coriander finely and place in a saucer for people to add to their bowls.

Pour the fish sauce into another saucer or small serving bowl. Finely chop the chillies and scatter them into the fish sauce.

Peel and then smash the garlic clove up using a pestle and mortar, or crush it, mix it with the lime juice and place in another saucer. Put the saucers on the table for people to help themselves.

1 litre (1¾ pints) chicken stock
1 celery stick, diced
2 slices of fresh root ginger, peeled
1 lemon grass stalk
300g (10½oz) cold leftover cooked rice
200g (7oz) minced chicken
pinch of salt
pinch of ground white pepper
bunch of fresh coriander
4 tbsp fish sauce
3 bird's eye chillies (fewer, if delicate)
1 garlic clove
juice of 3 limes

The Koreans and the Chinese both eat rice cakes, though in different shapes. The latter eat oval-shaped cakes, often found dried, usually around Chinese New Year for good fortune, while the Korean version is tube or pillow shaped and eaten far more frequently. Rice cakes are filling but they don't taste of anything, so are usually cooked with strong flavours; tteokbokki is a popular Korean street food and consists of rice cakes cooked with gochujang, which this recipe is based on. Here, I've added a couple of Western ingredients for maximum flavour.

KOREAN RICE CAKES with CHORIZO and GREENS

SERVES 4

If your rice cakes are dried, soak them in water for 24 hours before use. Bring a large saucepan of water to the boil, add the rice cakes and simmer for 3 minutes, then drain and rinse in cold water. Toss in the sesame oil.

Heat up a wok, add the cooking chorizo and fry the gently to release the oils. if it's looking dry, add the tablespoon of cooking oil. Add the yellow onion and fry gently until softened. Add the kimchi, garlic and gochujang, and fry well for a few minutes, then add the rice wine and the kale or cavolo nero. Fry gently for a further 10 minutes until the kale or cabbage is tender. Add the rice cakes, sugar and the stock or water and simmer over a low heat for a few more minutes. The dish will thicken with the addition of the rice cakes.

Take off the heat, stir in the spring onions and coriander and serve immediately.

400g (14oz) bag frozen rice cakes, in pillow shapes or dried discs *(see above)*

1 tbsp sesame oil

3 small hot cooking chorizo sausages, skinned and roughly chopped

1 tbsp cooking oil (optional)

1 yellow onion, sliced into thin half-moons

3 tbsp cabbage kimchi *(see page 143 for homemade)*, roughly chopped

2 garlic cloves, very finely chopped

1½ tbsp gochujang *(see page 16)*

2 tbsp Shaoxing rice wine

2 handfuls of kale or cavolo nero, roughly chopped

1 tsp sugar

150ml (5fl oz/¼pint) chicken stock or water

2 spring onions, diagonally sliced

small handful of fresh coriander leaves, roughly chopped

3 pandan leaves, tied in a knot, or **1 tsp** vanilla extract

100g (3½oz) black glutinous (sticky) rice, soaked in cold water overnight and drained

3 tbsp desiccated coconut

70g (2½oz) palm sugar

1 large ripe mango

150ml (5fl oz/¼ pint) coconut milk

3 tbsp pomegranate seeds

BLACK STICKY RICE
with MANGO

SERVES 4

The traditional Thai dessert is sticky rice with mango made with white glutinous rice, but this works equally well. The black glutinous rice makes a dramatic dish, especially when offset by the vibrancy of the colourful fruit. You can turn this into a breakfast or brunch dish by adding sunflower seeds, pumpkin seeds and orange segments. Experiment with different fruit, like strawberries, dragonfruit or blueberries.

Bring 500ml (18fl oz) of water to the boil in a large saucepan and add the pandan leaves or the vanilla extract. Add the rice and simmer for 40 minutes on a medium heat without the lid, stirring every 10 minutes, until the grains are soft and most of the water is absorbed. Some grains may have split, which is OK. Stir well and set to one side. If it's looking quite wet, drain off the water.

Meanwhile, toast the desiccated coconut in a nonstick dry frying pan on the lowest heat, stirring often, for 10 minutes until it is golden brown and crumbly. Grind in a food processor or spice or coffee grinder until it is a fine texture.

Heat up 200ml (7fl oz) water in a small saucepan and add the palm sugar, stirring until it has dissolved. Bring to a simmer on a medium heat and simmer for 5 minutes, then take off the heat, so that you have a rich syrup. Stir into the cooked rice.

Peel the mango skin away from the flesh and, using a sharp knife, cut the mango flesh into wedges from either side of the stone. Warm the coconut milk briefly in a small saucepan. To serve, divide the rice between 4 individual bowls and drizzle with the coconut milk. Place a few mango wedges on the side, then sprinkle with the pomegranate seeds. Lastly, sprinkle with a pinch or two of the toasted coconut.

I'm willing to wager that every Asian country has a variant of congee. It is porridge made from rice – by cooking it in a lot of water or stock, it breaks down to varying thicknesses, depending on which country you're from or what your preference is. The Cantonese (who call it jook) often favour a thick, wallpaper paste-like soup, creamy and without much differentiation in grains, while Teochew style is thinner, with the rice grains kept intact. It's usually a breakfast food, and often food for the infirm, the elderly and the young. The key to a good congee is either cooking it with lots of flavour (such as in stock made from chicken carcasses or pork bones), or serving it with lots of tasty things to add.

CONGEE

Wash the rice a couple of times, then drain. Add the rice to a saucepan with the water and bring to the boil. Simmer gently on a low heat with the lid half on for an hour, stirring a few times. If you like this consistency, remove from the heat. If you prefer a thicker, creamier style, cook for longer, stirring more often, until it has reached your desired consistency. If it becomes too thick, you can loosen it with a bit of water.

100g (3½oz) fragrant jasmine rice
850ml (1½ pints) water

SERVES 2

SUGGESTED ADDITIONS

Sometimes I eat congee for sustenance when I'm under the weather, in which case I prefer plain congee. Other times, when I want a full meal, I add one of the following:

Fish fillets or slices of pork fillet (1), marinated in a little soy sauce and cornflour and then cooked by swishing in the congee for 5 minutes until just cooked through.

Minced chicken (2), seasoned with white pepper, formed into balls and dropped into the congee to cook for 5 minutes.

Salted egg yolk (see page 163), steamed for 3 minutes and finely chopped.

POPULAR TOPPINGS

Nori (3) (see page 188), toasted under the grill until crisp and crumbled into flakes.

Pork scratchings (4) – yup, just bash them up a little and throw them in. Some go a little soggy and soft, while other bits retain crispiness; I love the contrasts.

Spring onion (5).

Fresh coriander. (6)

Fresh root ginger (7), cut into matchsticks and sizzled in 1 tbsp hot cooking oil.

Fish skin crisps (8).

Roasted peanuts (9).

Century egg (10) (see page 163), shelled and diced.

Toasted sesame seeds (11).

Preserved vegetable omelette (12) – cooked with a splash of fish sauce and Tianjin preserved vegetable (see page 162).

Pickles – spicy pickled turnip, pickled mustard green (see page 162).

Egg yolk, popped into a bowl of piping hot congee (the yolk will cook in the residual heat).

Poached egg.

Deep-fried dough stick – in Hong Kong and Taiwan, these savoury doughnuts are dipped into congee or soya milk. Heavenly.

I miss Malaysia. My trip there in April 2011 affected me greatly; it was one of the most hard-core eating trips I've done. After day 3 I forgot how it felt to be hungry and instead felt only 'full', 'really very full' and 'ohmygod-I'm-going-to-be-sick'. The ease of getting a quick bowl of noodles for next to nothing made me giddy and I hit the noodle soups hard, one of my favourites being Curry Mee. This thick, spicy and coconutty soup contained chunks of congealed pig's blood and little cockles, as well as tofu puffs and prawns. Alas, it's not as easy to get hold of pig's blood and cockles back home, so my version leaves these out (you may be relieved to hear).

MALAYSIAN CURRY MEE

400ml can coconut milk

250ml (9fl oz) chicken stock

4 fresh kaffir lime leaves

branch of fresh curry leaves

6 tofu puffs (*see page 128*), halved

100g (3½oz) fish cake (*see page 129*), thinly sliced

2 free-range eggs

handful of green beans

handful of bean sprouts

300g (10½oz) fresh yellow egg noodles

100g (3½oz) dried rice vermicelli, cooked and cooled

For the curry paste:

15 small purple shallots

7 garlic cloves

7.5cm (3in) piece of fresh root ginger, peeled

6 dried red chillies, soaked in just-boiled water for about 30 minutes until soft and then drained

4 lemon grass stalks, tender inner parts only

roots or stems of a bunch of fresh coriander

2 tsp ground coriander

1 tsp belacan (shrimp paste) (*see page 17*)

1 tsp sugar

vegetable oil, for blending and storing

To serve:

handful of fresh coriander

1 lime, quartered

sambal oelek

Chop all the paste ingredients roughly and then blend in a mini chopper or blender, adding some oil as you go to make a fine paste. Any leftover paste should be kept in a sterilized airtight jar with a film of oil on top in the fridge (it will keep OK for a week).

In a large saucepan, slowly fry 2 tablespoons curry paste per person, so 8 tablespoons in this instance, for 15 minutes. Add the coconut milk, the stock, lime leaves and curry leaf branch – keep the curry leaves on the branch, as this makes them easier to remove. Cover with a lid and simmer gently for 35 minutes. Add the tofu puffs for the last 15 minutes and the fish cake slices for the last 5, then take the pan off the heat. Remove the curry leaf branch.

Add the eggs to a saucepan of boiling water and cook for 6 minutes, then take off the heat, drain and run under cold water. Peel carefully.

In another saucepan of boiling water, simmer the green beans for 3 minutes, adding the bean sprouts to blanch for the final 30 seconds, then drain. Cook the egg noodles as per their packet instructions (mine required just plunging into boiling water for a couple of minutes) and drain.

To serve, divide the egg noodles and vermicelli noodles equally between 4 deep bowls. Top with the bean sprouts and green beans. Heat the soup base up until simmering, then distribute equally between the bowls. Halve each egg over the bowls and carefully place an egg half in each, then sprinkle the coriander on top and serve with a lime quarter per bowl, along with the sambal oelek.

Served cold, these noodles are warming, hearty and filling, the very antithesis of a limp, cold noodle salad. At a push you can use tahini in place of the dark sesame paste *(see page 17)*, but you won't get as rich a flavour. You can, however, use virtually any crunchy, sliced vegetable; I've made this with blanched broccoli, green beans and even red cabbage. When I'm trying to eat lighter, I up the vegetables and down the noodles, and it makes a great packed lunch with grilled chicken or salmon.

SESAME & PEANUT NOODLE SALAD

SERVES
4
AS A SIDE DISH

2 **tbsp** unsalted raw peanuts

1 **tbsp** white sesame seeds

1 large carrot, peeled and julienned

1 red pepper, cored, deseeded and thinly sliced into strips

handful of sugar snap peas, thinly sliced vertically

handful of bean sprouts

2 spring onions, greens parts only, julienned

200g (7oz) or **2 nests** of flat dried egg noodles

a few stalks of fresh coriander, roughly chopped, to garnish

For the dressing:

2 **tbsp** chunky peanut butter

3 **tbsp** dark sesame paste (see recipe introduction)

1 **tbsp** sesame oil

1 **tbsp** chilli oil

2 **tbsp** light soy sauce

2 **tbsp** warm water

1½ **tbsp** rice vinegar

1 **tsp** sugar

2.5cm (1in) piece of fresh root ginger, peeled and very finely chopped

1 large red chilli, very finely chopped

For the dressing, mix the peanut butter with the sesame paste, oils, soy sauce, warm water and vinegar. Add the sugar, ginger and chilli and mix thoroughly so that it becomes emulsified. This is easiest to do in a clean, empty jar with a tight-fitting lid; secure the lid and shake well.

Add the peanuts to a dry frying pan on a medium heat and toast for several minutes until golden but not burned, shaking the pan every so often. Remove and leave to cool, then chop roughly. Add the sesame seeds to the pan and toast until fragrant, shaking the pan often.

Add all your vegetables to a large bowl. Cook the egg noodles as per the package instructions and then drain and refresh under cold water so that they stop cooking and they don't stick together. Drain really well, then add to the vegetables. Add the dressing and get your hands in there, working the dressing into the mixture throughout. Garnish with the coriander and the toasted peanuts and sesame seeds.

This wouldn't be classed as one of the world's best-looking dishes, but mention it to any Chinese, Singaporean or Malaysian and a misty-eyed expression of homesickness will take over their faces. Ho fun noodles are essential for this – no other will do for that ultimate comfort of springy, satisfying rice noodles in a soothing, thick gravy.

SEAFOOD HO FUN IN EGG GRAVY

SERVES 2-3

Soak the ho fun in a bowl of hot water, separating the noodle strands carefully with your fingers. Drain and toss them with the dark soy sauce.

Heat 1 tablespoon of the cooking oil in a wok on a medium heat until it is shimmering. Add half the garlic and the noodles and stir-fry over a high heat to get some caramelization on the noodles for a couple of minutes. Remove to a serving dish and leave in a warm place.

Bring a saucepan of water to the boil. Using a slotted spoon, blanch the greens in the boiling water for 2 minutes and remove with a slotted spoon. Blanch the squid, prawns and the fish cake or balls for 2 minutes, then remove and place on top of the noodles with the greens.

Wipe the wok clean. Put back over a medium heat, add the remaining tablespoon of oil and fry the remaining garlic, the ginger and bacon together for 2–3 minutes. Add the stock, light soy sauce, white pepper, oyster sauce and sugar. Simmer for 3 minutes, then add the cornflour solution and cook until it has thickened to a roast dinner gravy-like consistency.

Turn the heat off and drizzle the beaten egg in, stirring as you go, so that you get strands of egg suspended in the sauce. Pour over the noodles and serve immediately, garnished with the spring onion.

1 packet (400g/13oz) fresh ho fun noodles (*see page 48*)

1 tbsp dark soy sauce

2 tbsp cooking oil

4 garlic cloves, very finely chopped

a few leaves of choy sum or other leafy green

1 small squid, cleaned and sliced into rings

10 uncooked peeled king prawns

½ fish cake, thinly sliced, or 6 fish balls, halved (*see page 129*)

1 tsp peeled and grated fresh root ginger

2 rashers of unsmoked streaky bacon, finely chopped

500ml (18fl oz) chicken stock

1½ tbsp light soy sauce

pinch of ground white pepper

1 tbsp oyster sauce

pinch of sugar

3 tbsp cornflour, mixed with **3 tbsp** cold water

2 free-range eggs, beaten

1 spring onion, finely chopped

Kway chap is the name of this Singaporean dish but also of the shape of the noodle. When dried, they are square or triangular-shaped flakes, but once you cook them, they become soft and often roll into a cigar shape, trapping the intensely spiced broth of this recipe within its folds. Traditionally, all sorts of piggy offal is simmered in the broth too, but as that's not entirely easy to find and also somewhat challenging, I've left it out.

KWAY CHAP

1 pork shank

1 tbsp cooking oil

6 star anise

7.5cm (3in) piece of fresh root ginger, peeled and whacked with the side of a knife

3 garlic cloves, lightly crushed

3 cinnamon sticks

5 cloves

1 bay leaf

1 black cardamom

4 tbsp light soy sauce

1 tbsp dark soy sauce

1 tbsp sugar

3 free-range eggs

8 tofu puffs (*see page 128*)

400g (14oz) dried rice flake noodles

2 tbsp Chinkiang black vinegar

10g (¼oz) yellow rock sugar

For the chilli & ginger sauce:

10 large red chillies

5cm (2in) piece of fresh root ginger, peeled and roughly chopped

pinch of salt

1 tsp water

Blanch the pork shank in a saucepan of boiling water for 3 minutes, then drain and rinse. Clean out the inside of the pan – this is so that you won't have to skim any scum off the broth.

Heat the oil in a large saucepan over a medium heat and fry the star anise, ginger, garlic, cinnamon sticks, cloves and bay leaf for 2 minutes, stirring all the while. Add the pork shank and black cardamom and then add the light soy sauce, dark soy sauce and sugar. Pour enough water into the saucepan to cover the pork shank, and turn the heat up to high. Once boiling, turn the heat down to low and place the lid on. Simmer very gently for 2 hours.

Meanwhile, cook the eggs in a saucepan of simmering water for 7 minutes. Drain the eggs and run under cold water, then shell them. Soak the tofu puffs in just-boiled water for 10 minutes, then squeeze the water out of them. Chop each in half.

Add the eggs and tofu puffs to the pan and simmer for another 30 minutes.

To make the chilli and ginger sauce to accompany the meal, deseed the chillies and chop roughly. Blend in a blender with the ginger, salt and water until smooth. Transfer to a serving bowl.

Bring a large saucepan of water to the boil. Add the rice flakes and cook for 5–8 minutes until soft. Drain and divide them between serving bowls.

To serve, fish the pork shank out of the broth and lay on a big plate. Fish out the eggs and halve them, arranging them around the pork shank, then do the same with the tofu puffs. Flavour the broth with the Chinkiang vinegar and yellow rock sugar, stirring over a low heat to dissolve, then ladle the spiced broth into the bowls with the noodles, avoiding the large spices. Serve the platter of meat with the chilli and ginger sauce for people to dip into.

This salad is everything I love about Thai food. Pretty on the plate, the flavours of the herbs make it refreshing and bright, and the lemon grass and lime leaves have an unparalleled fragrance. The noodles are slippery, but the minced pork and vegetables get caught up in their glassy tangles. It's not for the faint-hearted, so dial it down or deseed the chillies if you're feeding those of a delicate constitution. I make big batches of this for picnics or barbecues, as it works incredibly well cold or at room temperature.

THAI GLASS NOODLE
SALAD (YUM WOON SEN)

SERVES **4** AS A SIDE

If you're using mung bean noodles, leave the noodles to soak in tap-hot water for 10 minutes until tender. If you're using sweet potato noodles (which are a bit more robust), boil a kettle of water and pour over the noodles in a bowl, then leave them to soak for 15 minutes until tender.

Toast the peanuts and cashews in a dry frying pan over a low heat for about 10 minutes until golden, shaking the pan every so often so that they don't burn. Set aside.

Slice the red onion into half-moons and place in a bowl with the pinch of salt and the juice of 1 lime. Leave to soak for at least 15 minutes while you prepare the rest of the salad – this removes the harshness of the raw onion.

Drain the dried shrimps and pound using a pestle and mortar for 10 minutes until they have broken down into a mush. Chop the bird's eye chillies finely, then add to the shrimp, pounding a few times to amalgamate it. Add the sugar, fish sauce and the juice of the remaining lime, combining as you go. Taste the dressing – is it sour enough, sweet enough, savoury enough? – and adjust if necessary.

Add the celery and red pepper to a large bowl. Drain the noodles and rinse with cold water, then drain thoroughly and add to the bowl. Add the mint and coriander, tossing well so that everything is evenly distributed. Drain the red onions and rinse them, then add them too.

Heat the oil in a frying pan or wok over a high heat and fry the minced pork, breaking up any lumps. Add the lemon grass and sliced lime leaves and stir-fry until the pork takes on some colour. Add the prawns and stir-fry for a little longer until they are completely pink. Take off the heat and add to the bowl of noodles. Pour in the dressing and carefully toss together, using your hands once the pork has cooled a little. Finally, bash up the nuts using the pestle and mortar and garnish the salad with them.

200g (7oz) dried mung bean or sweet potato glass noodles (*see page 49*)

2 **tbsp** unsalted peanuts

2 **tbsp** unsalted cashews

1 **small** red onion

pinch of salt

juice of 2 limes

2 **tbsp** dried shrimps, washed and soaked in just-boiled water for 10 minutes

2 red bird's eye chillies

2 **tsp** sugar

4 **tbsp** fish sauce

1 celery stick, peeled and julienned

1 red pepper, cored, deseeded and julienned

3 **sprigs** of mint, leaves removed and roughly chopped

small handful of fresh coriander, roughly chopped

1 **tsp** cooking oil

250g (9oz) minced pork

1 lemon grass stalk, woody outer layers discarded, tender inner parts very finely chopped

3 kaffir lime leaves, rolled up and thinly sliced

10 large uncooked peeled prawns

It's not often I favour chicken over pork, but having tried this recipe in both guises, the lighter flavour of the chicken actually works better here and complements the pickled vegetables perfectly. Don't get me wrong – chicken will never steal my heart as pork does (I am part Chinese, after all), but pork is somehow too flavoursome here. This is a favourite of mine when I'm feeling under the weather; the silky slippery noodles are comforting, while the spicy sour flavours feel like they're doing battle in your body against whatever ails you.

HOT *and* SOUR CHICKEN NOODLES

SERVES
2

Soak the sweet potato noodles in boiling water as per the packet instructions until cooked. Meanwhile, skin and debone the chicken thighs. Put into a food processor with the ginger and pulse until coarsely minced.

Rinse the pickled vegetable and set to one side. Heat the cooking oil in a wok over a high heat, add the garlic, chicken mixture and the chillies and stir-fry until there is no pink left in the meat. Add the chilli bean paste and stir-fry until everything is coated. Throw in the pickled vegetable, soy sauce, vinegar, sugar and stock, and simmer for 10 minutes. Meanwhile, steam your vegetables for serving.

To assemble, place the noodles in the bowl and top with the vegetables. Add the chicken mixture on top with half the broth per bowl. Finally, drizzle the sesame oil on top and garnish with the spring onions.

150g (5½oz) dried sweet potato glass noodles (*see page 49*)

2 chicken thighs

2.5cm (1in) piece of fresh ginger root, peeled and roughly chopped

30g (1oz) sachet of ready-sliced Sichuan zha cai (*see page 162*), or any kind of pickled vegetable will do

1 tbsp cooking oil

3 garlic cloves, very finely chopped

2 long red chillies, finely chopped

2 tbsp chilli bean paste (*see page 16*)

1 tbsp light soy sauce

1 tbsp Chinkiang black vinegar

1 tsp sugar

300ml (10fl oz/½ pint) chicken stock

steamed pak choi, or any greens of your choice really (I used pak choi and sugar snap peas), to serve

1 tsp sesame oil

2 spring onions, diagonally sliced, to garnish

In Japanese, yaki means fried, and udon is a thick wheat noodle that stands up incredibly well to being fried at high heat due to its robust nature and satisfying chew. You can really use anything you have lying around for this recipe; when I'm down to odds and sods of vegetables left lying in the fridge, more often than not they will be sliced up and stir-fried in this manner. It's a filling and quick dish, a staple for busy weekdays when I don't have much time to cook.

YAKI UDON

SERVES 1

1 packet (200g/7oz) vacuum-packed or frozen udon

1 tbsp cooking oil

2 garlic cloves, very finely chopped

½ small white onion, thinly sliced into half-moons

2 stalks of Tenderstem broccoli

1 small carrot, peeled and julienned

100g (3½oz) boneless, skinless chicken breast, thinly sliced, or uncooked peeled prawns

handful of bean sprouts

1 Chinese or white cabbage leaf, rolled up and thinly sliced

1 tbsp mirin

1 tbsp light soy sauce

1 tsp pickled ginger, julienned (optional)

1 spring onion, green part only, diagonally sliced

1 tbsp dried bonito flakes (*see page 209*)

For vacuum-packed noodles, run them under warm water to loosen. If the noodles are frozen, soak them in boiling water until the strands loosen and then drain.

Heat the oil in a wok over a high heat. Add the noodles and garlic, followed by the onion, broccoli, carrot and chicken or prawns, and stir-fry briskly for 2–3 minutes. Add the bean sprouts, followed by the cabbage, and stir-fry for 2 minutes, then add the mirin and soy sauce and stir-fry for another minute.

Spoon out into a bowl or plate, topping with the spring onion greens and the pickled ginger, with the bonito flakes sprinkled over.

Traditionally, char siu (Cantonese roast pork) is made using pork tenderloin. But I find that fat is flavour when it comes to meat, so I much prefer to use shoulder; an inexpensive cut, interspersed with fat to keep it moist. These noodles need barely any cooking at all, since they're quite thin. A plunge in boiling water and a rinse in cold water to get rid of the starch and then a warm-up is all they really require to keep that essential bite and elasticity.

DRY-TOSSED CHAR SIU NOODLES

SERVES 2

500g (1lb 2oz) boneless pork shoulder steaks, cut into strips

2 tbsp clear honey

2 bundles of fresh wonton or Hong Kong noodles

For the marinade:

4 garlic cloves

large slice of fresh root ginger, peeled

2 tbsp hoi sin sauce

1 tbsp yellow bean paste (*see page 16*)

½ tsp DIY Five-spice Powder (*see page 205 for homemade*)

1 tsp sesame oil

1 tsp Shaoxing rice wine

For the sauce:

85g (3oz) spring onion

40g (1½ oz) fresh root ginger

pinch of salt

1 tbsp cooking oil

1 tbsp sesame oil

2 tbsp light soy sauce

1 tbsp oyster sauce

1 tsp rice vinegar

Mix the marinade ingredients together in a dish, add the pork shoulder strips and turn to coat in the mixture. Cover the dish with clingfilm and leave to marinate in the fridge overnight.

When coming to cook the pork, remove from the fridge and leave to come up to room temperature for an hour or so. Meanwhile, preheat the oven to 200°C (400°F) Gas Mark 6. Place the pork strips on a rack set over a roasting tray and roast for 40 minutes, turning them once halfway through the cooking time. Decant the juices from the roasting tray and mix with the honey. Brush the pork shoulder strips with this and roast for a further 5 minutes. Remove and leave to rest in a warm place for 15 minutes.

Meanwhile, for the sauce, slice the spring onion finely and peel and very finely chop the ginger. Place in a bowl with the rest of the sauce ingredients. Stir well to combine and set aside for at least 10 minutes so that all the flavours have time to mix.

Bring a large saucepan of water to the boil, and put a colander in the sink. Place the bundles of noodles in the boiling water for 30 seconds, then transfer to the colander with a slotted spoon, reserving the boiling water. Wash the noodles under cold water – this gets rid of the excess starch on the noodles. Just before serving, plunge the noodles back into the water for another 30 seconds before draining and tossing with the ginger and spring onion sauce. Chop the char siu and serve on top of the noodles.

4 rashers of streaky bacon, chopped into small pieces

½ **sheet** of nori (*see page 188*), toasted under the grill until crisp

1 small head of purple sprouting broccoli or any other dark leafy green

1 spring onion

1 fat garlic clove

2 **handfuls** of grated Parmesan cheese

2 free-range egg yolks

2 x 200g (7oz) **blocks** of vacuum-packed or frozen udon

freshly ground black pepper

UDON CARBONARA

SERVES

2

This is an enormous bastardization of the classic Italian carbonara. Traditionalists will wince, Italians might issue death threats, but I am pushing on with – dare I say it – fusion. Udon is the perfect noodle for this; thick, worm-like, chewy and slippery, it is much more satisfying than spaghetti. The creamy, cheesy sauce clings to each strand like a sexy hug. I've Asian-ed it with the addition of spring onion and toasted nori, the latter of which adds another whack to an already umami-packed dish.

Fry the bacon in a nonstick frying pan over a medium heat until most of the fat has rendered and the bacon is starting to crisp.

While the bacon is frying, scrunch the nori in your hands into a bowl so that it becomes large flakes/dust. Separate the broccoli into small florets, trimming away any old tough bits. Separate the white part of the spring onion and shred finely, reserving and very finely chopping the green part for garnish.

Crush the garlic, add to the bacon pan and fry gently on a low heat for a couple of minutes. Add the whites of the spring onion, then immediately take off the heat.

Whisk the Parmesan with the egg yolks in a large bowl. Bring a saucepan of water to the boil and cook the broccoli or leafy greens for 1 minute, then add the udon and cook as per the packet instructions (usually about 3 minutes, or until the blocks have loosened and untangled). Reserve 4 tablespoons of the cooking water, then drain the noodles well and add to the egg and cheese mixture. Add the bacon mixture and toss well with the reserved cooking water. The egg and Parmesan mixture will emulsify into a sauce, coating the udon strands as you keep mixing. Garnish with the spring onion greens, toasted nori and plenty of black pepper, then serve immediately on warmed plates.

A cold noodle soup, especially an icy, sour one, might be an alien concept that takes getting used to, but it's perfect for a hot summer's day. The buckwheat noodles in this preparation are chewy and elastic, giving you a proper pull from the bowl.

KOREAN SUMMERTIME NOODLES (MUL NAENGMYEON)

SERVES 2

Rinse the beef brisket under cold running water. Bring the water to the boil in a large saucepan with the anchovies, shiitake mushrooms and kombu. Boil on a high heat for 15 minutes, then add the beef brisket and simmer over a gentle heat with the lid on for 40 minutes.

Remove the beef and set to one side, then drain the stock through a fine sieve into a large bowl. Discard the kombu, anchovies and mushrooms. Season the broth with the salt, sugar and vinegar, then taste – it should be quite tangy. Leave to cool and then place in the freezer for a minimum of 30 minutes, but a maximum of 1 hour – it should be a slushy liquid when serving, not solid.

Bring a large saucepan of water to the boil, add the noodles and cook for 3–5 minutes, or according to the packet instructions. Drain well and then plunge into cold water. Drain again, and plunge back into fresh cold water.

Slice the halves from the pear either side of the core, then cut them into thin slices. Slice the beef brisket as thinly as you can, and slice the cucumber into thin half-moons.

To assemble the noodles, pour half the cold broth into each of 2 serving bowls. Add a tangle of noodles and top with a few slices of the brisket. Top with 3 slices of the pear and a few of the cucumber half-moons, followed by a hard-boiled egg half. Top this with the spring onion greens. Add a pile of kimchi on top of the noodles to the side and sprinkle each bowl with the toasted sesame seeds. Smear half a teaspoon of English mustard on to the inside lip of each bowl so that the eater can dab as they see fit.

150g (5½oz) beef brisket
700ml (1¼ pints) water
8 dried anchovies, heads pinched off
2 dried shiitake mushrooms
piece of dried kombu (see page 188), about 7.5 x 13cm (3 x 5in)
½ tsp salt
pinch of sugar
1 tbsp rice vinegar
250g (9oz) Korean buckwheat noodles
1 Asian pear
1 small cucumber
1 free-range hard-boiled egg, shelled and halved
1 spring onion, green part only, julienned
2 tbsp radish kimchi (chong gak) or cabbage kimchi (see page 143 for homemade)
1 tbsp white sesame seeds, toasted
1 tsp English mustard

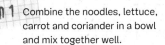
01 Combine the noodles, lettuce, carrot and coriander in a bowl and mix together well.

Mix the sauce ingredients together in a suitable bowl until well combined.

Prepare a bowl of hand-hot water. Lay out a clean, dry tea towel in front of you.

Dip a wrapper in the water and leave for a few seconds – it should start softening up. Remove from the water and lay out flat on the tea towel.

Add about 2 tablespoons of the filling to the centre of the wrapper but slightly nearer the bottom closest to you. Top with a tablespoon of crab or pork etc (if using).

VIETNAMESE SUMMER ROLLS

Rice paper is the Vietnamese version of a spring roll wrapper. Sold dried in rounds, rice paper is brittle and fragile when dry, yet supple and elastic once softened in water. Summer rolls use the rice paper in its softened state, while spring rolls go a step further with a little deep-frying action.

20g (¾oz) **bundle** of dried rice vermicelli noodles, soaked in just-boiled water for 8 minutes and then drained, rinsed and cut into 7.5cm (3in) lengths

1 small head of Little Gem lettuce, shredded

1 carrot, peeled and julienned

100g (3½oz) picked white crab meat or leftover cooked shredded pork, chicken or duck (optional)

small handful of fresh coriander, finely chopped

10–15 summer roll wrappers (skins)

10 large cooked peeled prawns, sliced in half lengthways

a few sprigs of mint, leaves picked

bundle of chives

For the dipping sauce:

2 **tbsp** hoi sin sauce

1 **tbsp** Homemade Sriracha (*see page 109, or use shop-bought*) or chilli oil

1 **tsp** smooth peanut butter

1 **tbsp** rice vinegar

½ **tbsp** water

Fold the bottom flap over the filling, tucking it under the filling a little.

Then fold the 2 sides in tightly.

Add a couple of mint leaves and line up 3 prawn halves horizontally in a row on the empty wrapper above the filling,

Place seam side down, under a damp tea towel, while you prepare the rest.

Serve the rolls with the dipping sauce, or alternatively with Nuoc Cham (see page 34).

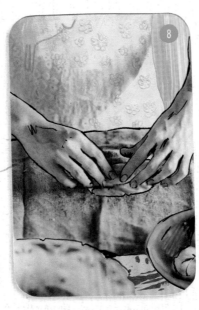

Fold the whole thing over again. The wrapper should be tacky enough to stick to itself.

Place a couple of chives so that they sit in line horizontally with the pouch of filling but so that they will poke out of the side.

These differ from summer rolls slightly, besides the obvious method of cooking. The fresh herbs are replaced with garlic and shallots, the salad vegetables with cooking vegetables and the salad is served on the side for you to wrap your spring roll up in and dip in the sauce, almost like an inside-out roll. I prefer these with glass noodles rather than rice vermicelli, as they withstand the deep-frying better.

VIETNAMESE SPRING ROLLS

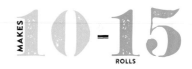

MAKES 10-15 ROLLS

Mix the minced pork with the wood ear mushrooms, garlic and shallots. Add the sugar and stir to combine.

Heat a wok with 1 tablespoon of the cooking oil and fry the pork mixture until it is no longer raw. Remove and leave to cool. Combine with the noodles and carrot in a bowl.

Meanwhile, prepare a bowl of hand-hot water. Lay out a clean, dry tea towel in front of you. Dip a summer roll wrapper in the water and leave for a few seconds – it should start softening up. Remove from the water and lay out flat on the tea towel. Add about 2 tablespoons of the filling to the centre of the wrapper but slightly nearer the bottom closest to you. Fold the bottom flap over the filling, tucking it under the filling a little, then fold the 2 sides in tightly and fold the whole thing over again. The wrapper should be tacky enough to stick to itself. Place on a plate, seam side down, under a damp tea towel while you prepare the rest.

Preheat the oven to 110°C (225°F) Gas Mark 1/4. Wipe the wok out with kitchen paper and add the remaining cooking oil. Heat to 180°C (350°F), or until bubbles appear up the sides of a wooden chopstick when inserted into the hot oil. Fry the spring rolls, in batches, for 6 or so minutes, turning once if the oil doesn't cover them, until they have bubbled and are golden brown. Remove with a slotted spoon and leave to drain on a wire rack set over a baking sheet in the oven while you fry the rest.

Serve with nuoc cham and whole lettuce leaves with mint and Thai basil leaves for people to help themselves.

100g (3½oz) minced pork

1 dried wood ear mushroom, soaked in just-boiled water for 30 minutes and then drained, rolled up and shredded

3 garlic cloves, very finely chopped

3 shallots, finely sliced

1 tsp sugar

200ml (7fl oz) cooking oil

100g (3½oz) dried glass noodles (*see page 49*), soaked in just-boiled water for 5 minutes, drained, then rinsed and cut into 7.5cm (3in) lengths

1 carrot, peeled and julienned

10–15 summer roll wrappers (skins)

To serve

Nuoc Cham (*see page 34*)

whole lettuce leaves

mint leaves

Thai basil leaves

This is one of my favourite Vietnamese noodle dishes. When I'm after something a little more substantial, I use Jiangxi noodles, the thicker version of the 'bun' type, almost spaghetti-like in thickness. When I want a lighter meal, I'll plump for vermicelli. Crisp, crunchy vegetables give the impression of a healthy meal, even if I do then go and top it with something deep-fried, but you can also use grilled pork, or lemon grass-marinated chicken instead. Usually served at room temperature, they also make a great packed lunch. Just go easy on the garlic in the nuoc cham if you're using it, unless you have very forgiving colleagues.

VIETNAMESE SPRING ROLL NOODLES

SERVES 1

100g (3½oz) dried rice vermicelli or Jiangxi noodles (*see page 48*), the former soaked in just-boiled water for 10 minutes and drained, the latter soaked for 30 minutes and drained

½ small cucumber, peeled and sliced into half-moons

1 small carrot, peeled and shredded

1 Little Gem or Iceberg lettuce leaf, finely sliced

a few sprigs of fresh coriander, roughly chopped

1 sprig of mint, leaves picked and thinly sliced

1 quantity Nuoc Cham (*see page 34*)

2 Vietnamese Spring Rolls (*see opposite*)

Place the noodles in a bundle in the middle of your bowl, and line one edge with the half-moons of cucumber. Arrange little piles of carrot and lettuce on top of the noodles, and scatter with the herbs.

Drizzle the nuoc cham over, then top with the spring rolls. To eat, stir and toss everything with chopsticks to amalgamate.

INSTANT NOODLE PIMPS

Like any good Asian kid, I love instant noodles. I grew up with them. I'm not talking Pot Noodles, oh no, these are way better. Sometimes in life, you may not have the time or inclination to cook a big meal. Whatever the reason, enjoy those instant noodles. There are hundreds of varieties. Experiment and embellish them. Here's a little help with that.

NOODLES

There are so many brands of instant noodle that it could take a lifetime to try them all. There are your standard ramen blocks with soup sachets, then there are types that are to be served dressed rather than in soup and there are those that come in their own cup. Experiment with them, have a play and figure out your favourite.

STOCK

First things first. You can throw that flavouring sachet away and make these with chicken stock, or add soy sauce, sesame oil or fish sauce to water. But let's face it, the sachets are easy. They're tasty. Instant noodles come in so many flavours now that you can, for example, match a seafood one to one you'll pimp with prawns, for example.

MEAT

You can, really, go for any meat. Leftover roasted meats, raw meat sliced thinly and swooshed in the stock to cook, uncooked prawns, fish fillets, smoked pork sausages, frankfurters, SPAM – it all works. You can even use canned sardines in tomato sauce, warmed though with a little chilli oil, to dress the noodles rather than having them in soup.

EGGS

Top your noodles with a fried egg, or a soft-boiled egg, or crack an egg into the broth to poach while the noodles are cooking too. Place an egg in a metal container with a lid (like a small saucepan) with just-boiled water for 10 minutes for an onsen tamago (hot spring egg), where the egg white is slightly floppy and the yolk firmer.

HERBS & AROMATICS

Coriander and spring onion are king. Slivered fresh kaffir lime leaves added to the broth works a treat too. A squeeze of lime juice goes a long way, and you can also buy tubs of fried shallots to sprinkle on top. Basil, Vietnamese hot mint (rau ram), perilla leaves and dill also work well when used with appropriate flavours – beef stock with basil and hot mint, for instance, like a faux pho.

VEGETABLES

Pretty essential these. Pak choi, choi sum, gai laan, sugar snap peas, mangetout, green beans, chicory, Tenderstem broccoli, chard, spinach, watercress, baby corn, quartered tomatoes, bean sprouts and Iceberg or Cos (Romaine) lettuce all work marvellously and will cook happily in the broth with the noodles.

GARNISHES

You may have noticed that I like chillies rather a lot. So I almost always have some form of chilli going, and with noodles it's no exception. Sliced rings of chilli, chilli oil, Tabasco, sriracha (*see page 109 for homemade, or use shop-bought*), Chilli & Ginger Sauce (*see page 64*), chopped chillies in a little rice vinegar, Nuoc Cham (*see page 34*) and nam prik pao (a Thai roasted chilli paste) are all winners.

This is the ultimate instant noodle pimp. It's filthy. It was developed after the Korean War when the Koreans used store-cupboard ingredients left behind on US military bases. Canned meats and processed cheese are the main ingredients for this stew; embrace it in its guilty glory, especially if you're hungover or attempting to survive the apocalypse and you happen to have a working gas stove.

BUDDAE JJIGAE

SERVES 2

1 tbsp sesame oil

1 tsp very finely chopped garlic

2 tbsp gochujang (*see page 16*)

50g (1¾oz) cabbage kimchi (*see page 143 for homemade*), roughly chopped

3 spring onions, white parts sliced into 3cm (1¼in) lengths, green parts thinly sliced diagonally

2 frankfurters (preferably the jarred type in brine), sliced diagonally into thick slices

175g (6oz) tinned SPAM, sliced into thick slices

200g (7oz) canned baked beans

750ml (1¼ pints) water

1 packet (75g/3oz) instant ramen (*see page 49*)

2 processed cheese slices

Heat up a saucepan or clay pot (*see page 11*) with the sesame oil and fry the garlic over a low heat for 30 seconds until fragrant.

Add the gochujang and mix well. Add the kimchi, the whites of the spring onions, the frankfurters, SPAM and the baked beans, then the water – try and keep each component in a different part of the pan so that it's like a layered casserole. Next, add the instant ramen block and submerge it in liquid, then put the lid on to simmer for 4 minutes.

Remove the lid and wiggle a fork around the noodles to loosen. If it's looking a little dry, add a touch more water. Finally, add the cheese slices on top and put the lid back on for a minute so that they melt. To serve, scatter the spring onion greens on top.

CHAPTER

3

VEGETABLES & FRUIT

VEGETABLES & FRUIT

The fruit and vegetable department of the Asian supermarket is often bewildering, mainly because green leafy vegetables can look very similar, and they are usually labelled with their Chinese/Thai/Vietnamese names, depending on the specialism of the supermarket you are in. Some don't even have English names. If in doubt, as a general rule, I wash them well and stir-fry them with garlic until I've worked out what they are. Hopefully, the images here will help you work them out.

HERBS & AROMATICS

Lemon grass, galangal and kaffir lime leaves are the holy trinity of Thai cooking. Coriander, mint, Thai basil, Vietnamese coriander, pandan leaves and betel leaves are also worth exploring.

SHISO LEAVES

Shiso leaves are commonly used in Korean and Japanese cuisine. Also called perilla, they have a medicinal fragrance, a little minty, with a hint of aniseed.

VEGETABLES

ALLIUMS

Chinese chives, flowering chives, garlic scapes and spring onions all belong to this same family, Allium, but range from being very onion-like in flavour to being closer to garlic. The stems of each have a different shape that suits different uses. Chinese chives (also called garlic chives) are flat, for example, and are often used to flavour dumplings and breads, whereas garlic scapes (also known as sprouts or ramps) have round cylindrical stems and are more often used as a vegetable in their own right, as are flowering chives.

(1, 2 & 3) MELONS & GOURDS

Although winter melon (1) and bitter melon (2) are both called melons, they couldn't be further from each other taste-wise. One is soft and inoffensive, the other bitter and aggressive. The loofah gourd (3), however, is wonderfully spongy, as you might imagine from its name.

(4) MOOLI
(DAIKON OR ASIAN RADISH)

You can pickle it, eat it raw, braise it and even make it into a cake – truly, the most versatile of the vegetables.

(5) LOTUS ROOTS

Lotus roots are visually stunning, with the arrangement of holes through the root. They don't taste of much, but provide a texture. They must always be cooked, as they are not safe to eat raw.

FRESH MUSHROOMS

Enoki, shimeji and king oyster mushrooms are the main varieties available. While enoki and shimeji are delicate and require only a little cooking, the king oyster is meaty and robust.

LEAFY GREENS

(6) CHINESE CABBAGE
(CHINESE LEAF OR NAPA CABBAGE)

Large and pale green or yellow in colour, this is eaten raw or cooked, and is often used to make kimchi too.

(7) CHINESE BROCCOLI
(KAI LAAN)

Dark green with a long, thick stem and a small broccoli-like head on top, sometimes with small yellow flowers, Chinese broccoli is iron-rich in flavour and often steamed or stir-fried.

(8) PAK CHOI

This comes in green and white varieties, and large and baby forms, and is often steamed or stir-fried.

(9) CHOI SUM

Like pak choi, but longer-stemmed and thinner, choi sum is stir-fried, steamed or served in noodle soups.

(10) WATER SPINACH
(TUNG CHOI OR KANG KONG)

These long, arrow-shaped leaves with long stems that are round and hollow are usually stir-fried with pungent flavourings.

(11) PEA SHOOTS
(DOU MIU)

With short, squat, rounded leaves, pea shoots are usually stir-fried but sometimes served in soups.

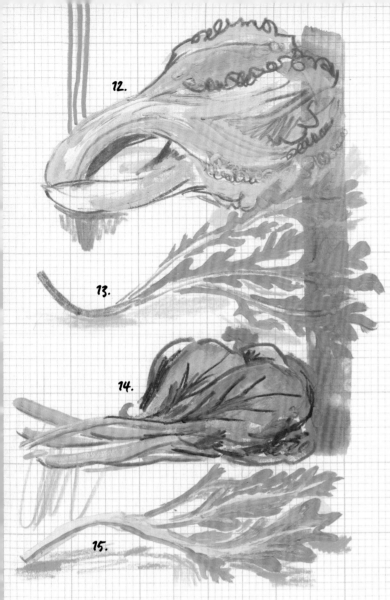

12.

13.

14.

15.

(12) MUSTARD GREENS (GAI CHOY)

These are what you would find pickled (*see page 162*). They have a bit of a spicy bite to them. You can pickle them yourself, braise them or add them to soups.

(13) CHRYSANTHEMUM GREENS (TONG HO)

These flat, rounded leaves are slightly bitter and medicinal in flavour, and are often used in hot pots and soups.

(14) RED / GREEN AMARANTH

The red amaranth leaves are easily distinguishable, since they have a red tinge on the underside of the leaf. Sturdy and iron-rich, the green version is often used in soups, though the red is reserved for stir-frying, as the colour inside them releases a vibrant pink juice.

(15) MIZUNA

Used mostly in Japanese cooking, mizuna leaves are delicate and long, and spiked at the edges. They taste a bit like rocket.

HOW I LIKE TO EAT LEAFY GREENS

In Soup (noodle soup, broths, stews): Chinese cabbage, pea shoots, chrysanthemum greens, pak choi, choi sum, mustard greens, green amaranth, mizuna

Stir-fried with ginger: Chinese broccoli (boil in water with 1 tsp sugar for 2 minutes, then stir-fry)

Stir-fried with garlic: Pea shoots, pak choi, Chinese cabbage, red / green amaranth

Stir-fried with garlic & fermented bean curd: Water spinach, Chinese broccoli (boil in water with 1 tsp sugar for 2 minutes, then stir-fry)

Steamed & drizzled with oyster sauce: Pak choi, choi sum, Chinese broccoli

Raw: Chinese cabbage, mizuna

FRUIT

(16) MANGOSTEEN

Often called the 'queen of fruits', mangosteens are little purple spheres and are one of my favourite fruits. Squeeze the rind until the fruit splits, then pull apart to reveal the soft white flesh inside. The larger globes may have a seed in them which you can spit out. Soft, creamy and fragrant, these don't come cheap when imported, but are incredibly delicious.

(17) RAMBUTAN

These are distinctive from their red, hairy outer shells. Crack the skin open and pop the fruit in your mouth, but there is a seed in the centre you will need to spit out.

(18) LONGANS

Called 'dragon's eye' in Cantonese, these are similar in size to lychees, but are beige and smooth-skinned. Pop the skin open with your teeth after washing them, then peel the skin away to reveal the flesh.

(19) LYCHEES

Pink-skinned and a little knobbly, lychees need to be peeled before eating and stoned. Purée the fruit and reduce to a syrup to flavour drinks, or ice the lychee flesh and eat with ice cream.

(20) ASIAN PEARS

These are yellow and round; the skin is thin and the flesh has an almost icy texture to it. Not a great deal of flavour other than sweetness, but one of my trusted hangover alleviators.

(21) DRAGONFRUIT

It's a dramatic-looking fruit, with pink skin and black-seeded, snow-white flesh. The skin should not be eaten. To prepare, slice the fruit in half and scoop the white flesh out with a large spoon.

(22) PAPAYA

Long and oval-shaped, ripe papayas are orange-fleshed. They're my least favourite fruit; they're a bit too reminiscent of rotting fruit. I can just about bear them with a squeeze of lime. To make classic Thai salads, go for unripe and green fruits.

(23) MANGO

Mangoes are now so easily available you can buy them in most general supermarkets. Alphonso mangos, available for a short season, are some of the best; honey-like in flavour and creamy. Many Indian and Caribbean grocers sell mango purée in tins.

(24) DURIAN

Often called the 'king of fruits', durian is infamous for its god-awful smell. Banned in many hotels and public transport in Asia, durian is pretty good once you get past the odour. The fruit itself is encased in a hard, spiked shell; once you get it open, bright yellow lobes of creamy flesh can be eaten, made into ice cream, cakes and candies. You will often find the lobes frozen or in the fridge section of the supermarket.

16. 17. 18. 19. 20. 21. 22. 23. 24.

Tom yum is a classic Thai soup; it's a light, bright and spicy broth made by simmering aromatic herbs and chillies. The key components – lemon grass, galangal and kaffir lime leaves – are completely essential to the flavour of this. Don't be tempted to replace the water with chicken stock, as it's not supposed to taste of chicken. It should be fragrant from the citrus. Coconut water was a trick I picked up from my travels in Thailand; it adds depth and sweetness without being overpowering. The brilliant thing is that all the flavourings can be kept in the freezer, so tom yum is at hand as long as you have a couple of vegetables and a lime.

SERVES

2

AS A STARTER OR LIGHT MEAL

TOM YUM GOONG

400ml (14fl oz) water

200ml (7fl oz) coconut water (NOT coconut milk) – you can buy coconut water in cartons, such as Vita Coco; go for the unflavoured, 100% natural variety (optional)

2 red bird's eye chillies (more if you're a chilli fiend), snapped in half

3 slices of fresh galangal, peeled

5 kaffir lime leaves

2 lemon grass stalks, woody outer layers removed

6 cherry tomatoes

handful of fresh oyster mushrooms, washed and roughly torn

6 large uncooked prawns in their shells, defrosted in cold water if frozen

1 tsp nam prik pao (Thai roasted chilli paste)

1 lime, halved, for juicing

2 tbsp fish sauce

a few sprigs of fresh coriander, roughly chopped

Simmer the water and coconut water in a saucepan with the chillies, galangal, 2 of the lime leaves and the lemon grass for 20 minutes with the lid on. Strain the stock through a sieve to get rid of the bits.

Add the cherry tomatoes and mushrooms and simmer over a medium heat for 3 minutes, then add the prawns and the remaining lime leaves, torn in half. Bring to a simmer, then take the pan off the heat. Leave to stand for 5 minutes, then stir in the nam prik pao.

To each bowl, add the juice of half a lime and 1 tablespoon of the fish sauce. Pour the soup into the bowls and toss the coriander on top. It's a spicy soup, so reduce the number of chillies in the soup if you can't take the heat.

➺ OTHER IDEAS

Replace 300ml (10fl oz / ½ pint) of the water with coconut milk to make the richer Tom Kha Goong.

Lemon grass has a special kind of flavour that you can't really substitute with anything else. It has a floral, citrus fragrance to it, deliciously perfumed. It goes very well with seafood, and these mussels are creamy and rich, filling but delicate. Lemon grass keeps very well in the freezer.

MUSSELS IN LEMON GRASS BROTH

SERVES 2 OR 1
AS A STARTER
AS A MAIN

Check over the mussels, throwing out any with damaged shells or any open ones that won't shut after tapping them lightly on a hard surface. Pull away the stringy beards and scrape off any barnacles with a knife, then rinse well.

Heat the cooking oil with the garlic in a saucepan on a medium heat until fragrant but not browned. Add the coconut milk and water and bring to the boil. Add the woody outer layers of the lemon grass stalks and simmer for 10 minutes on a medium-low heat, covered with the lid.

Meanwhile, bash the finely chopped lemon grass inner parts with a pestle and mortar to release their fragrance. Add the sugar, grated lime rind and fish sauce, mixing well. Fish the lemon grass outer layers from the coconut milk mixture and discard, then add the chillies and lime leaves.

Add the mussels to the coconut milk mixture, turn the heat up to medium and put the lid on. Cook for 3–5 minutes, stirring once – they are ready when all the shells have opened up (discard any that have failed to open). Take off the heat and add the sugar, lemon grass and fish sauce mixture with the shallot, then put the lid back on for another minute.

Dish out into 2 deep bowls, scatter the coriander on top and squeeze over the lime juice before serving. You can add some pre-cooked rice vermicelli to the bottom of each bowl before serving for a more substantial meal.

400g (14oz) live mussels

1 tbsp cooking oil

2 garlic cloves, very finely chopped

200ml (7fl oz) canned coconut milk

100ml (3½fl oz) water

2 lemon grass stalks, woody outer layers removed but reserved, tender inner parts finely chopped

1 tsp caster sugar

grated rind and juice of ½ lime

1½ tbsp fish sauce

2 red bird's eye chillies, broken in half

3 kaffir lime leaves

1 red Asian shallot or banana shallot, finely sliced

handful of fresh coriander, roughly chopped

Cabbage. Cabbage. Not exactly a sexy word, is it? To most, cabbage evokes memories of an over-cooked pile of sludge at school dinners, but this dish is anything but. Bright green leaves stir-fried to just tender are perked up with this tangy sauce.

CABBAGE IN VINEGAR SAUCE

SERVES 4 WITH OTHER DISHES

Mix all the sauce ingredients together and set aside.

Bring a saucepan of water to the boil and blanch the Chinese cabbage in it for 1 minute, then drain well.

While the cabbage is still hot, heat the oil in a wok and fry the Sichuan peppercorns until the oil is fragrant, then remove them with a slotted spoon. Then fry the dried chillies until they are brown but not burned. Add the ginger, garlic and spring onion whites, and stir-fry briefly. Add the blanched cabbage and stir-fry until heated through. You want to do this at a high heat to get some smoky flavour into the vegetables. Add the sauce and stir-fry until the sauce has thickened.

Place the vegetables on a plate and garnish with the spring onion greens.

about 600g (1lb 5oz) Chinese cabbage (Chinese leaf or Napa cabbage)

2–3 tbsp cooking oil

2 tsp Sichuan peppercorns

a few dried chillies, deseeded and cut into small pieces

small piece of fresh root ginger, peeled and finely chopped

3 garlic cloves, very finely chopped

1 heaped tbsp chopped spring onion, white parts only, green parts reserved and finely sliced

For the sauce:

2½ tbsp Chinkiang black vinegar or other good-quality Chinese vinegar

1 tbsp sugar

½ tsp salt

2 tsp light soy sauce

1 rounded tsp cornflour

1 tbsp cold water

Garlic scapes (also called sprouts or ramps) are the sturdiest of the allium family that you can find in Chinatown. The stems are round and thick, smelling pungently of garlic that mellows out in cooking, and can take a fair bit of heat. If you can't find them, use spring onions or Chinese chives instead (*see page 82*), and reduce the cooking time.

SERVES

2

AS A SIDE
DISH

GARLIC SCAPES STIR-FRIED
with PRAWNS *&* EGG

Mix the soy sauce with the cornflour in a bowl, stir in the prawns and leave to marinate while you prepare the rest of the dish.

Beat the eggs in another bowl with the black pepper, white pepper, salt and rice wine. Cut the garlic scapes into 4cm (1½in) lengths.

Heat a wok on a medium heat and swirl 1 tablespoon of the cooking oil around it. When it is shimmering, add the garlic scapes and stir-fry for a good 5 minutes so that they take on some colour and soften. Turn the heat up to max and add the prawns, stir-frying them with the scapes for 30 seconds so that they turn a little pink. Push to one side and add the remaining tablespoon of cooking oil.

Pour in the eggs and leave for 10 seconds to set, then scramble into the prawns and scapes with a spatula. Take off the heat so that the eggs remain soft and creamy, then serve with some rice or noodles.

1 tsp light soy sauce

1 tsp cornflour

200g (7oz) uncooked peeled king prawns

4 free-range eggs

pinch of ground black pepper

pinch of ground white pepper

pinch of salt

1 tbsp Shaoxing rice wine

4 stalks of garlic scapes

2 tbsp cooking oil

splash of sesame oil

↠OTHER IDEAS

Stir-fry the garlic scapes with thinly sliced marinated meat, tofu (bean curd) or mushrooms, make pesto with them or shred them raw and add to the dressing for the Smacked Cucumber Salad (see page 33).

There is just a hint of seasoning here, since the garlic scapes and the bacon are so aromatic on their own. The garlic scapes are like a grassy, sweeter garlic and are robust when raw; mellow when cooked. I especially enjoy the flavour of them when they are a little charred. Like a lot of dishes in Asian cuisines, just a little bit of meat is needed to impart flavour rather than to dominate. I often eat this with just a bowl of rice.

SERVES 4 AS A SIDE DISH

THAI-STYLE GARLIC SCAPES STIR-FRIED *with* BACON

400g (14oz) garlic scapes (sprouts) (*see page 82*)
6 rashers of smoked streaky bacon
1 tbsp cooking oil
1 tbsp fish sauce
1 tsp sugar
½ tsp ground white pepper

Wash your garlic scapes thoroughly, pat dry with kitchen paper and then chop into 5cm (2in) lengths. Slice the bacon rashers into slivers.

Heat the oil in a wok on a high heat until just below smoking. Add the bacon and stir-fry until some of the fat has rendered and the bacon is starting to crisp.

Turn the heat up to max and add the garlic scapes. Stir-fry briskly for 3 minutes, then add the fish sauce, sugar and white pepper. Stir-fry for another minute, then take off the heat and spoon out on to a plate.

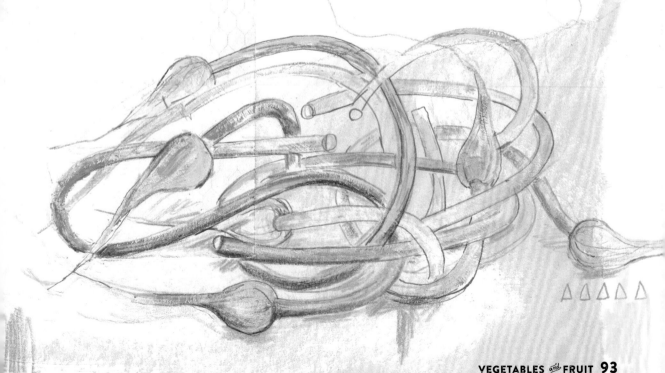

These are called 'bing' and are sold all over China in various forms from the street. A popular version is made with egg instead of a pancake – the egg is poured over a hot plate and spread out until wafer thin, then topped with spring onions and other flavourings, before it's folded within itself to make a parcel. I prefer these breads (often called pancakes), for they are able to soak up that delicious sauce far more easily. You will often see these made with spring onions, especially in America, but Chinese chives are brilliant here too, as they are mellower and sweeter.

CHINESE CHIVE BREADS

SERVES 4 - 6 AS A SNACK

Add the flour and salt to a large mixing bowl. Add the just-boiled water to the flour, bit by bit, mixing with a wooden spoon. Leave to cool for 10 minutes. Transfer to a floured work surface and knead the dough for 3 minutes until it is smooth and silky. Place back in the bowl, cover with a clean tea towel and leave for 30 minutes.

Meanwhile, slice your chives or spring onions very finely. Mix all the ingredients for the dipping sauce together in an appropriate bowl.

At this point you may need to set your oven on to warm the breads, as they will need to be cooked 1–2 at a time.

Separate the dough into 4 pieces. Dust your work surface with flour.

160g (5¾ oz) strong white flour, plus extra for dusting
½ tsp salt
80ml (3fl oz) just-boiled water
large bunch of Chinese chives or spring onions
3 tbsp toasted sesame oil
2 tbsp cooking oil

For the dipping sauce:
1 tbsp chilli oil with sediment (*see page 12*)
2 tbsp light soy sauce
2 tbsp Chinkiang black vinegar
1 tsp sugar
a few slivers of julienned fresh root ginger

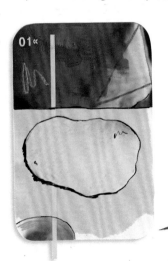

Roll 1 piece of dough out into a large circle about 3mm (⅛in) thick.

Brush one side with a little of the sesame oil

Roll up into a cigar from the bottom upwards.

Coil the dough around tightly into a snail shape

Flatten each coil, then roll out into a large circle.

Brush again with sesame oil and scatter with a quarter of the chives or spring onions.

Repeat the cigar rolling and the snail coiling and then carefully roll out again.

The chives (or spring onions) will burst out of the dough a little, but this isn't a bad thing.

9 Repeat with the other 3 pieces of dough, separating them with a piece of greaseproof paper so that they don't stick together.

Heat up 1 tablespoon of the cooking oil in a nonstick or cast-iron frying pan to a medium heat. Fry a pancake on one side, pressing down any layers that have puffed up with a spatula, until golden and crisp. Turn over and repeat. Add the second tablespoon of cooking oil to the pan after you've fried the second pancake.

Slice each pancake into quarters and serve with the dipping sauce.

250g (9oz) fresh winter melon

1 tbsp dried shrimps

2 tbsp cooking oil

1 spring onion, diagonally sliced,
white and green parts separated

1 tbsp peeled and chopped fresh root ginger

large pinch of salt

50ml (2fl oz) water

pinch of ground white pepper

WINTER MELON BRAISED *with* DRIED SHRIMPS

Winter melon, used most often in soups, tastes of very little, so one might ask why we don't just feed it to the pigs? Because it has a wonderful texture that is light and non-fibrous, and it has a way of soaking up all the flavours around it.

Peel the winter melon using a vegetable peeler, then cut into thick matchsticks.

Wash the dried shrimps and then soak in a bowl of hot water for 2 minutes. Drain and leave to one side.

Heat a wok up on a high heat and add the cooking oil, swirling it to coat the sides. Add the whites of the spring onion and the ginger and stir-fry over the high heat for about 20 seconds until fragrant. Add the soaked shrimps and winter melon sticks and stir-fry for 2 minutes.

Add the salt, water and white pepper and stir-fry until the water has evaporated. Turn off the heat and taste to check the seasoning, then serve in deep bowls garnished with the sliced spring onion greens.

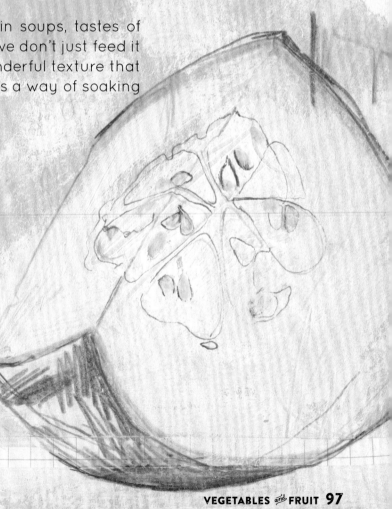

Bitter melon is something of an acquired taste. Chances are you might hate it. But you might love it, especially if you drink Guinness or bitter. It's a bit of a unique vegetable in that respect; we usually prize sweetness in vegetables and fruit, but this is the exact opposite. Look for bright, light green melons, as these tend to be less aggressively bitter. The Indian equivalent is darker green and knobbly, called kerala, and is much more bitter in flavour. It is believed that bitter melon has a blood glucose-lowering effect, though this is probably negated by how much sugar I like in the sauce.

BITTER MELON STUFFED
with PORK & PRAWN

SERVES

1 bitter melon

3 tbsp salt

75g (2¾oz) minced pork

75g (2¾oz) uncooked peeled prawns, very finely chopped

1 spring onion, finely sliced

1 tsp peeled and grated fresh root ginger

½ dried wood ear mushroom, soaked in just-boiled water for 30 minutes and then drained, then curled into a cigar shape and thinly sliced

1 tsp cornflour

½ tbsp light soy sauce

1 tsp sesame oil

1 tbsp cooking oil

For the sauce:

300ml (10fl oz/½ pint) water

1 tbsp sugar

2 tbsp oyster sauce

1 tbsp light soy sauce

1 tsp cornflour, mixed with **1 tbsp** cold water

Slice the bitter melon into rounds about 4cm (1½ in) wide. Use a teaspoon to scrape the inside membrane and seeds out. Boil a little water and dissolve the salt in it in a large bowl, then fill up with enough cold water to cover the bitter melon rounds. Leave to soak for 30 minutes – this reduces the bitterness.

Meanwhile, mix the pork, prawns, spring onion, ginger, mushroom, cornflour, soy sauce and sesame oil well with your hands in a separate bowl. Cover with clingfilm and leave to marinate while the bitter melon is soaking.

Drain the bitter melon and pat dry with kitchen paper, then stuff with the pork and prawn mixture. Add the cooking oil to a wok and heat on a medium heat for 1 minute. Fry the bitter melon rounds on one side for 4 minutes until golden browned, then flip and fry on the other side for another 4 minutes.

For the sauce, mix the water, sugar, oyster sauce and soy sauce together and add to the wok. Place the lid on and cook on a medium heat for 10 minutes. Add the cornflour solution to the wok to thicken the sauce; this shouldn't take more than a couple of minutes. Remove the bitter melon to a dish, drizzle the sauce on top and serve with steamed rice.

⇥ OTHER IDEAS

Stir-fry bitter melon with pork and soy sauce, cook it in black bean sauce or, if you're a real sadist, juice it.

2 rounds 3cm (1¼in) wide cut from a large, peeled mooli (daikon), plus an additional slice for garnish

2 dried shiitake mushrooms, soaked in just-boiled water for 30 minutes and then drained

600ml (20fl oz/1 pint) dashi (*see page 209 for homemade*)

1 tbsp mirin

1 tbsp light soy sauce

1 spring onion, green part only, julienned

JAPANESE SIMMERED MOOLI

This dish celebrates the purest flavour of the Asian radish, mooli (also called daikon). I eat this dish a lot when I'm craving lighter meals – with a bit of rice and some stir-fried vegetables, you'll feel positively saintly after this. For a fuller meal, you can add chicken drumsticks to simmer in the broth first.

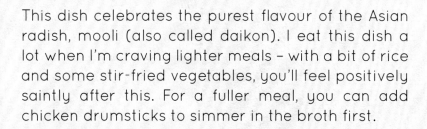

➥ OTHER IDEAS
You can flavour this further by adding marinated slices of fish to top the mooli rounds and steam briefly with the lid on.

Cut a cross into each mooli round about half their width deep. Remove the stems from the shiitake mushrooms and add to the dashi in a saucepan, then add the mooli, cut side down, with the mirin and soy sauce. Bring the dashi to the boil, then turn the heat down and simmer gently for 20 minutes with the lid cocked. Turn the mooli slices over and simmer for a further 20 minutes.

To serve, add a slice of mooli to a bowl and fish out a mushroom. Place the mushroom, cap side up, in the bowl. Grate the additional mooli slice on the finest grater of the box, then mix 1 teaspoon of it with half the julienned spring onion greens and pile into a mushroom cap. If your mushroom is a little small, it won't hurt if it overflows. Repeat with the rest of the grated mooli and spring onion greens and the remaining mushroom. Spoon the dashi stock around the mooli rounds.

The incredibly versatile mooli (daikon) is used in many countries. You will often see it finely grated to accompany sushi, stewed in meaty broths and even curried. Long, white and slender, when raw it is crisp with a mild pepperiness, and is excellent julienned in slaws. Its sturdy structure means that it can also be slow-cooked in stews without breaking down, and one of the most famous uses for it is in this turnip 'cake' – a steamed dish that, once cooled, is then fried until crispy on both sides. It's classic Cantonese, eaten often at dim sum and celebrations such as Chinese New Year, though the carrot is my addition; I like it for its sweetness and colour.

TURNIP CAKE (LOH BAK GOH)

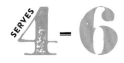
SERVES 4-6

500g (1lb 2oz) mooli (daikon), peeled

2 carrots, peeled

1½ tsp salt

1½ tbsp sugar

1 scant tsp ground white pepper

4 tbsp cooking oil, plus extra for oiling

5 shallots, thinly sliced

3 garlic cloves, very finely chopped

2 Chinese sausages, diced

4 dried shiitake mushrooms, soaked in just-boiled water for 30 minutes, then drained, stems discarded and diced

1 tbsp dried shrimps, washed, soaked in just-boiled water for 15 minutes, then drained, squeezed dry and roughly chopped

3 tbsp Shaoxing rice wine

200g (7oz) rice flour (not glutinous)

30g (1oz) potato starch

6 spring onions, finely sliced

To serve

soy sauce

chilli oil

Using a box grater, grate a third of the mooli on the coarse setting into a saucepan, before grating the rest finely. This is to give the cake a little texture. Grate the carrots finely into the saucepan too and add 200ml (7fl oz) of water, along with the salt, sugar and white pepper. Simmer for 5–10 minutes on a medium heat until the vegetable matter is soft and the pan is quite dry.

Heat 1 tablespoon of the cooking oil in another saucepan over a medium heat and fry the shallots and garlic for 30 seconds, ensuring that they don't colour. Add the Chinese sausage and cook for 5 minutes so that all the fats in the sausage are released. Add the shiitake mushrooms and the dried shrimps, then add the rice wine and cover immediately. Steam like this for a couple of minutes, then remove the lid and cook, stirring, until the wine has evaporated. Remove from the heat.

Oil a loaf tin or a shallow baking tin. Whisk the rice flour and potato starch with 500ml (18fl oz) water in a large mixing bowl. Add the spring onions, meat mixture and the cooked mooli and carrot, mixing well. Add another 2 tablespoons of the cooking oil. Pour into the oiled tin and steam for 1 hour in a metal steamer, or in a larger baking tin filled with boiling water and covered in foil in an oven preheated to 150°C (300°F) Gas Mark 2. The cake will still have a wobbly centre. Leave to cool completely and then chill for a couple of hours.

To serve, heat the remaining tablespoon of cooking oil in a nonstick frying pan on a medium heat. Run a knife around the edge of the cake and turn out on to a plate. Cut slices as thick as your forefinger and fry on a medium heat for a few minutes on each side to form a golden brown crust. Serve with soy sauce and chilli oil.

1 loofah gourd, ridges cut off and peeled
1 tbsp cooking oil
2 garlic cloves, very finely chopped
1 bird's eye chilli, roughly chopped
handful of fresh oyster or shiitake mushrooms
1 tbsp light soy sauce
1 tbsp oyster sauce
½ tsp sugar
50ml (2fl oz) water
4 kaffir lime leaves, tough stems removed, rolled and very thinly sliced

LOOFAH GOURD STIR-FRIED *with* KAFFIR LIME LEAVES

SERVES 2 AS A SIDE DISH

Loofah gourds are also called luffa, or angled or ridged gourds due to their appearance. They are long and dark green, fatter at one end and thinning into a point at the other. The skin is best peeled off – cut down the ridges with a knife before peeling with a vegetable peeler – as it can be quite tough and bitter. The gourd is eaten when green and young; it's only when it becomes aged and fibrous that you should consider using it as a body scrubber (don't actually – they're processed first!). Keep the spongy innards and the seeds, as these are edible and make up the body of them. They taste mildly of cucumber, a little sweet, and soak up flavours beautifully when you stir-fry them or cook them in soups. This recipe uses the fragrance of kaffir lime leaves to give a normal vegetable side a new dimension.

Roll cut your loofah gourd: hold it in front of you and make the first cut at a 45° angle. Roll the loofah 90° away from you and cut again, repeating until you get to the end – this is so that it has the maximum surface area.

Heat up the cooking oil in a wok to just below smoking, then reduce the heat to medium, add the garlic and chilli and stir-fry briskly for 30 seconds. Turn the heat up high and add the loofah gourd and mushrooms, stir-frying as you go.

Add the soy sauce, oyster sauce and sugar and stir so that everything is well coated. Add the water, cover the wok and steam for 2 minutes so that the loofah becomes tender. Remove the lid, throw in the lime leaves and stir-fry for another minute so that the mixture is fairly dry but glossy and not sticking to the pan. Spoon out into a serving dish.

OTHER IDEAS

Stir-fry the gourd with scrambled eggs, curry it with tomatoes and Indian spices or pair it with tofu puffs and egg gravy (see Seafood Ho Fun in Egg Gravy, page 63).

Lotus root must always be cooked, as it's not safe to eat raw, and I know that deep-frying isn't something you should do all the time, but I tried these baked and they're... different. Tougher. Much like when you buy 'healthy' crisps in the hope that they will taste just as good as regular crisps and all they taste of is over-crunchiness and disappointment. So plough on with the deep-frying and eat a carrot stick to assuage the guilt. (That's how it works, right?) You can try a variety of seasonings, as long as they are dry, as anything wet will make them soggy, but any mix should have some salt in it for essential seasoning.

LOTUS ROOT CRISPS

1 tsp distilled white vinegar

1 lotus root

300ml (10fl oz/½ pint) vegetable oil, for deep-frying

For the seasoning:

3 parts fine table salt

1 part chilli flakes

2 parts nori (*see page 188*), toasted under the grill until crisp and crumbled into flakes

2 parts white sesame seeds, toasted, mixed with **1 part** sugar

Add the vinegar to a large bowl of water. Using a mandolin, slice the lotus root 2mm (1/16 in) thick and carefully place in the water to soak for 10 minutes. The vinegar prevents discolouration.

Grind the seasoning ingredients together using a pestle and mortar and have to hand. Pour the oil for deep-frying into a wok or large saucepan and heat to 180°C/350°F, or until bubbles appear up the sides of a wooden chopstick when inserted into the hot oil. Meanwhile, drain the lotus root slices and dry on kitchen paper thoroughly. Set up a wire rack over a plate nearby.

Deep-fry the lotus root slices for 3–5 minutes – they should be turning golden – in batches, so that the oil temperature doesn't drop too much. Remove the crisps with a slotted spoon and sprinkle with the seasoning generously before placing on the wire rack. Leave to cool and then serve. These will keep for 2 days in an airtight container.

Mushrooms like shimeji (both brown and white) and enoki are very delicate compared to the more robust shiitake and king oyster mushrooms, and indeed Western closed cup and chestnut varieties. The shimejis have a firm and slightly crunchy texture when cooked, and as such they work well in stir-fried dishes and soups. The brown have a slightly nuttier flavour compared to the white, but really when I'm selecting which is best for a dish it is often led by aesthetics.

STIR-FRIED SHIMEJI *and* KALE *with* BUTTER SOY SAUCE

Wash the mushrooms and slice across the base where the stems clump together. Separate the mushrooms carefully with your hands into small clusters.

Heat the oil in a wok to just below smoking. Add the kale or other greens and a splash of water and place the lid on to steam for a couple of minutes until the leaves are tender. Remove the lid and stir until any remaining moisture has evaporated, push the greens to one side of the wok and then turn the heat up to maximum. Immediately add the mushrooms and leave to sear for 30 seconds, then stir the mushrooms, add the butter and stir-fry for another 30 seconds. Add the soy sauce, stir-fry for 30 seconds and then take off the heat. Scatter with the snipped chives to garnish.

1 punnet of fresh white beech (bunapi) shimeji mushrooms

1 punnet of fresh brown beech (buna) shimeji mushrooms

1 tbsp cooking oil

handful of kale, cavolo nero or spring greens, washed and finely sliced

20g (¾oz) butter

1 tbsp soy sauce

small bundle of chives, snipped into 1cm (½in) lengths, to garnish

SERVES 2 AS A SIDE DISH

This is a great master teriyaki sauce recipe – salmon and chicken are particularly good with it, but the meatiness of king oyster mushrooms means that they completely absorb the flavour. Slightly smoky and unexpectedly rich, I don't see this as a vegetarian alternative; it's completely satisfying in its own right.

GRIDDLED TERIYAKI KING OYSTER MUSHROOMS

Slice the king oyster mushrooms lengthways 5mm (¼in) thick. Lay them out in a dish so that none overlap. Whisk the mirin, soy sauce, sake and sugar together, then pour over the mushrooms. Leave to marinate for an hour.

Preheat a cast-iron griddle pan until smoking. Turn the heat down to medium. Shake the marinade from the mushrooms, reserving the marinade, and brush with the cooking oil. Cook in one layer for 3 minutes, then turn 90 degrees so that you get crisscross griddle patterns. Turn over and repeat.

Meanwhile, simmer the remaining marinade in a saucepan for 30 seconds.

Place the mushrooms in a serving dish and drizzle the remaining marinade over them. Top with the julienned spring onion in a pile and drizzle the lemon juice over.

3 fresh king oyster mushrooms
1 tbsp mirin
50ml (2fl oz) light soy sauce
3 tbsp sake
1 tsp caster sugar
1 tbsp cooking oil
1 spring onion, julienned
1 tsp lemon juice

SERVES

2

Sriracha is an incredibly popular chilli sauce, originally from a province in Thailand. It's one of the milder chilli sauces, which might be why it has gained such popularity – it's not going to flame your face off. Due to the garlic content, this sauce is best suited to meals post-10am, but really it goes with anything. Make sure you use the large, slender chillies, like jalapeño or serrano, as if you were to make this with bird's eye it would be inedibly spicy. This makes a small pot's worth, so you may want to double or triple the recipe if you're a real fan of the sauce.

HOMEMADE SRIRACHA

Discard the stems of the chillies and chop roughly. Blend in a blender with the garlic, sugar, salt and water to a very fine paste. Place in a clean jar with a loose lid and leave it in a dark warm-ish place for 3 days (a kitchen cupboard is perfect). This is so that the chillies can start fermenting with the sugar and salt. After a couple of days you'll see bubbles starting to form.

Add the vinegar, then pour into a small saucepan and simmer on a medium heat for 15 or so minutes so that it thickens a little. Leave to cool, then blitz again with a stick blender. Strain through a fine sieve into a bowl to get rid of the pulp and seeds, then spoon into a sterilized glass jar to keep in the fridge for up to 1 month. It will thicken on cooling.

350g (12oz) large red chillies
1 garlic clove, peeled
2 tbsp dark soft brown sugar
1 tbsp salt
40ml (1½fl oz) water
70ml (2½fl oz) cider vinegar

MAKES

1 SMALL JAR

Pomelo is a beast – it looks like an enormous grapefruit, and I suppose that is essentially what it is; the segments within the fruit are looser and more defined, but it shares that sweet/sour/bitter flavour, perfect for pairing with a rich fish such as salmon. Look for yellow pomelos to signify ripeness, but of course you can use grapefruit in its place.

THAI CRISPY-SKINNED SALMON & POMELO SALAD

SERVES 2

1 salmon fillet (about 250–300g/8–10oz), skin on

1 tsp cooking oil

100g (3½oz) pomelo flesh, broken into small chunks

handful of bean sprouts, blanched and drained

4 red Asian shallots, thinly sliced

½ cucumber, soft insides scooped out and discarded, cut into matchsticks

2 kaffir lime leaves, stems removed, rolled into a cigar shape and thinly sliced

1 sprig of mint, leaves picked, rolled into a cigar shape and thinly sliced

a few sprigs of fresh coriander, roughly chopped

1 lemon grass stalk, woody outer layers removed

1 bird's eye chilli

juice of 1 lime

2 tsp sugar

1 tbsp fish sauce

Rub the salmon fillet with the oil and place in a cold, nonstick frying pan, skin side down. Slowly bring up to a high heat – this is to crisp the skin up. Once the skin is sizzling, turn the heat down to medium and check the salmon frequently until it is golden brown and crisp. Flip the salmon fillet and cook for 30 seconds (or a minute if you have a very thick fillet), then take off the heat and leave to rest in the pan.

Combine the pomelo with the bean sprouts, shallots, cucumber, lime leaves, mint and coriander in a large mixing bowl.

Slice the lemon grass core into very thin rounds, add to a mortar and bash with a pestle a couple of times, then add the bird's eye chilli and bash a few times more. You want to release the flavour but not pulverize it. Add the lime juice, sugar and fish sauce and stir to combine.

Remove the skin from the salmon fillet and set aside, then break the salmon into large chunks with your hands and add to the salad. Add the dressing and toss through your hands a few times, then scoop it out into a serving dish. To serve, crack the salmon skin into a few pieces and lay it on top.

This is a take on a classic Hong Kong dessert, often served in dim sum restaurants. It's a cold dish, refreshing for a hot day and light enough to eat after a rich meal. The pomelo, especially, gives short sharp bursts of acid, contrasting with the sweetness of the mango. You can buy sweetened mango purée in cans at Indian shops and some supermarkets, which is ideal; otherwise, make the purée from the fresh fruit with a little water and sugar added until it's the consistency of clear honey.

SAGO WITH POMELO *and* COCONUT

 SERVES 4

85g (3oz) tapioca pearls
2 tbsp caster sugar
150ml (5fl oz/¼ pint) coconut milk
pinch of salt
350ml (12fl oz) mango purée
1 mango, sliced down either side of the stone and flesh cubed
100g (3½oz) pomelo flesh
½ lime, for squeezing

Add the tapioca to a large saucepan filled with plenty of boiling water. Boil for 10 minutes with the lid on, stirring a couple of times, then take off the heat and leave it to stand for another 10 minutes so that it's completely translucent and soft.

Stir the sugar into the coconut milk until dissolved. Drain the tapioca into a sieve and rinse well to get rid of the excess starch, then add to the coconut milk immediately with the salt, stir well and place in the fridge until you are ready to serve. Don't leave it hanging around in the sieve or it will stick to it.

Add 3 tablespoons of the tapioca mixture to each of 4 small cocktail glasses or bowls. Then add 6 tablespoons mango purée to float on top of each, followed by the diced mango and pomelo flesh. Spritz with a little squirt of lime juice.

1 large green unripe mango, or ½ unripe papaya

½ garlic clove, peeled

small handful of dried shrimps, washed

1 tsp palm sugar, or to taste

juice of ½ lime

2 bird's eye chillies, or to taste

2 snake beans or **4** green beans, cut into 3cm (1¼in) sticks

1 tbsp roasted peanuts

1–2 tbsp fish sauce

5 cherry tomatoes

GREEN MANGO SALAD (SOM TAM)

SERVES 2

If you have wandered around Bangkok at any point, you will be familiar with the rhythmic pounding sound of pestle on mortar, as ladies sit by the roadside selling this salad, called som tam. Som tam is one spicy mother of a salad, made by pounding vegetables. Even if you refuse the chillies they hold up at you, there is still enough residual fire in those mortars from previous customers to make a face-melting difference. Unripe mangos or papaya are perfect for it, as they are a little tart but robust enough to deal with the classic pounding action that is required of this dish. Once your fruit becomes riper, it's best to do something else with it, as it will simply turn to mush.

Peel your mango (or papaya), discarding the stone (or seeds), and julienne the flesh – a julienne peeler is a wonderful and inexpensive investment.

Throw the garlic into a mortar and pound to a paste with a pestle. Add the dried shrimps and give them a pounding. Add the sugar, lime juice and whole chillies and give them a quick bash. Add the beans, peanuts and half the julienned mango (or papaya with 1 tablespoon fish sauce. Give the mixture a good bashing, then mix it together with the rest of the julienned mango (or papaya).

At this point, taste it to see if it needs any more fish sauce or sugar. It should be face-crunchingly spicy. Smash the tomatoes (shield yourself against squirtage) in the mortar, then add to the mango (or papaya) mixture. Serve with some steamed glutinous (sticky) rice.

OTHER IDEAS

If you can't get hold of unripe mango or papaya, try making the salad with a combination of carrot and mooli (daikon), or even cucumber.

Tamarind is a tree fruit that's used in cuisines all over the world. Mexicans make it into a drink (tamarindo), which I like with a drop of mezcal in it. The Thais use tamarind in cooking a lot, as do the Indians, and it's also used in Africa, where the tree originates. British Worcestershire and HP sauces contain tamarind too. It has a specific fruity sourness that is more mellow than citrus. This is traditionally made with crab in Vietnam, but because I'm a show-off and mainly because I like lobster more, I've used that instead. This is a really messy one; have finger bowls and napkins at the ready.

SERVES 2

LOBSTER IN TAMARIND SAUCE

65g (2½oz) chunk from a block of tamarind with seeds

300ml (10fl oz/½ pint) just-boiled water

1 live lobster, about 800g–1kg /1lb 12oz–2lb 4oz, placed in the freezer for 20 minutes

2 tbsp fish sauce

40g (1½oz) palm sugar, or to taste

1 tbsp Shaoxing rice wine

1 tbsp cooking oil

3 garlic cloves, very finely chopped

1 large red chilli, roughly chopped

½ tsp ground white pepper

3 spring onions, white parts sliced into 7.5cm (3in) sections, green parts finely sliced

½ tbsp cornflour, mixed with **2 tbsp** cold water

Place the tamarind chunk in a saucepan with the just-boiled water to cover it. Use a fork or spoon to work the tamarind flesh away from the seeds. This will take about 10 minutes. Once the liquid is cool enough, use your fingers to continue to work away the flesh and let it dissolve in the liquid. Strain through a sieve, reserving the water.

Bring a large saucepan of water to the boil. Add the frozen lobster, put the lid on and boil for 4 minutes, then remove the lobster and leave to cool for 10 minutes. Using a tea towel to protect your hands, remove the elastic bands on the lobster's claws. Lay the lobster out on a chopping board, hold the body with one hand and twist the claws off with the other. Separate the body from the tail by twisting and pulling it apart with your hands. Chop the tail across the width into 3 bits. Using a sharp knife, cut down lengthways through the head. There will be greenish liquid goo – this is the brains, and perfectly safe to eat. Scoop into a bowl. Chop through the base of the claws, then crack the claws using the base of a sharp knife tapped once just under the lobster claw joint so that the sauce can get to the meat.

Mix the tamarind water, fish sauce, sugar, rice wine and 2 tablespoons of water together. Heat in a saucepan over a medium heat until simmering and stir for a couple of minutes or so until the sugar dissolves. Taste for the sweet and sour balance, adding more tamarind water if it isn't sour enough, or more sugar if it's too sour. Add the green lobster goo and mix well.

Heat the cooking oil in a wok over a medium heat. Add the garlic and chilli so that they sizzle and stir-fry for 30 seconds. Add the lobster pieces and tamarind mixture, then add the white pepper and the whites of the spring onions, stir and cover with the lid. Simmer with the lid on for 3 minutes, stir, then add the cornflour solution and simmer for a further 2 minutes with the lid on until the lobster is cooked through and the sauce is glossy. Remove the lid, garnish with the greens of the spring onion and serve with vegetables and steamed rice or slices of baguette to dip in the sauce.

This tart is a classic preparation that has been 'Asianified' with the inclusion of coconut and some of the fruits you'll find at an Asian supermarket. While the tart is pretty, it also allows the flavour of the fruits to come through fairly unadulterated. One thing to note is that for a successful crème pâtissière free from lumps, you must whisk the shit out of it. I speak from experience.

MANGOSTEEN, DRAGONFRUIT & KIWI TART *with* COCONUT CREAM

For the pastry:

250g (9oz) plain flour, plus extra for dusting

50g (1¾oz) icing sugar

pinch of salt

finely grated rind of **1** orange

1 free-range egg yolk, beaten

125g (4½oz) cold unsalted butter, cut into cubes

50ml (2fl oz) ice-cold water

For the crème pâtissière:

4 free-range egg yolks

60g (2¼oz) caster sugar

15g (½oz) plain flour

15g (½oz) cornflour

350ml (12fl oz) coconut milk

For the topping:

4 strawberries, hulled and finely sliced

1 kiwi fruit, peeled and finely sliced

2 mangosteens, stems removed, then split to remove the globes of white, creamy fruit

1 dragonfruit, halved, flesh scooped out and sliced

50g (1¾oz) blueberries

2 tbsp peach or apricot jam

1 tbsp just-boiled water

Sift the flour and icing sugar for the pastry into a large mixing bowl, then stir in the salt and the orange rind. Add the egg yolk and mix well, then add the butter cubes and rub into the flour mixture with your fingers until it resembles breadcrumbs. Add 2 tablespoons of the iced water and mix until you get a loose dough; you may not need all the water. Once the dough comes together, clingfilm it and whack it in the fridge for at least half an hour.

For the crème pâtissière, place the egg yolks, sugar and both flours in an electric mixer or a large bowl and whisk for about 10 minutes until smooth, pale and creamy. Heat the coconut milk in a saucepan until it boils, then take off the heat and leave to cool for 30 seconds.

Preheat the oven to 200°C (400°F) Gas Mark 6. Pour half the coconut milk into the egg and sugar mixture while whisking at a high speed for 5 minutes. Pour the mixture back into the saucepan with the rest of the coconut milk over a medium heat, whisking all the while with a hand whisk. Heat until simmering – at this point it should be thickening rapidly. You want it to resemble a stiff jam. Take off the heat, leave to cool for 10 minutes, then cover with clingfilm touching the top of the crème pâtissière. Place in a sink full of cold water, but not so that the saucepan floats. Cool completely.

Meanwhile, lightly dust a work surface with flour. Roll your pastry out to 1cm (½in) thick, so that there is enough to line a 22cm (8½in) springform tart tin or quiche tin and overlap the edges a little. There may be an excess – this can be frozen to be used another time. Carefully place the pastry in your tart tin, pushing it down on to the base and into the edges. Cut greaseproof paper out to fit inside the tart case and around the edges and add ceramic baking beans. Bake for 15–20 minutes, so that the pastry is browned and crisp. Remove from the oven, lift the paper and beans out of the pastry case and leave to cool in the tin on a wire rack.

To assemble, spoon the crème pâtissière into the pastry case so that it comes two-thirds of the way up the sides. Decorate the tart as you wish with the prepared fruit and blueberries. Lastly, mix the jam with the just-boiled water to loosen and use to lightly glaze the fruit and the pastry crust. Leave to cool before serving.

HOW TO PREPARE PINEAPPLE *the* ASIAN WAY

The pineapple is an interesting fruit; it is one of the rare ones that works in both sweet and savoury dishes. There's an enzyme in pineapple that tenderizes meat, which is why it sometimes tickles your tongue when you bite into it; it is, effectively, biting you back. If you've ever been to Thailand or the Philippines or indeed Mexico, you might, as I was, be blown away by the skill and dexterity with which the street vendors strip a pineapple of its skin and eyes to create chunks of sweet, juicy fruit ready to eat without having to spit anything out or have any of it stuck in your teeth. A few sharp hacks of a large knife (or a machete, but let's stick to a knife) is all it takes.

In choosing your pineapple, give it a good sniff at the base of the fruit. People may look at you askance, but a ripe pineapple will smell so. Also, give the green leaves nearest the centre of the fruit a little tug; a ripe fruit will release them easily.

Stand the pineapple upright and, starting 5cm (2in) from the top of the green leaves, slice the skin off close to the flesh to reveal the 'eyes' all the way round.

Holding the pineapple with your left hand, you will see that the eyes sit in a diagonal row. Make an incision with your knife at a 45-degree angle from below the outer edge of 2–3 of the eyes, and repeat on the upper side so that the eyes come away cleanly. Repeat down the pineapple to the base, then turn the pineapple round and repeat until all the eyes have been cut out. Eventually the starting point will meet the end.

Cut the quarters in half, and then slice out the tough, woody centre. It's now ready to eat, or you can cut it into smaller bite-sized pieces.

Now take the top and bottom off. Rinse the pineapple, then cut it in half lengthways and then in half again.

This chilli, sugar and salt dip comes in a little bag with fruit purchased from street vendors in Thailand. It's fantastic with very sweet fruit, but also with acidic fruit like green apple, as the sugar balances it out a little. Green mango, pineapple, cantaloupe melon and watermelon work really well with this, and sometimes I crush in a few mint leaves for a little variation.

CHILLI SUGAR SALT DIP

1 large red chilli
1 tbsp fine salt
2 tbsp caster sugar

Slice the chilli in half lengthways and scoop the seeds out with a teaspoon. Slice thinly into half rings and place in a mortar. Add the salt and sugar and pound lightly with a pestle, tainting the sugar and salt mixture pink.

Durian smells awful. It smells like something died in stagnant water while wearing a teenage boy's football socks. Even the fruit itself doesn't look inviting, given the spikes it's covered in. But if you can get past that, it has a wonderfully creamy, custard texture and a fragrance in its flavour, if not smell.

DURIAN ICE CREAM

SERVES 4–6

Remove the flesh from the pieces of durian. There is usually a hard seed in the middle of each piece, which you should discard. Place the fruit in a blender. Add the rest of the ingredients and blend until smooth.

Pour into an ice-cream maker and churn/freeze according to the manufacturer's instructions. Alternatively, pour into a freezer-proof container and freeze for a couple of hours until almost frozen. Blend again to break down the ice crystals, then return to the freezer. You will have to repeat this process 3–4 times until the ice cream freezes smooth.

2 large pieces of durian (you can find this in the fridge or sometimes freezer section of the Asian supermarket)
370ml (12½fl oz) evaporated milk
250ml (9fl oz) whipping cream
85g (3oz) caster sugar
pinch of salt

On many roadsides in Thailand, a roti vendor will be slapping dough out deftly, chopping fruits or even egg into the dough being cooked on a hot plate for a snack or dessert. Crisp, crunchy pastry with just-warm bananas drizzled with condensed milk is my absolute favourite. Don't worry if you can't quite get the dough-slapping right – practice makes perfect.

MAKES 8

BANANA ROTIS

2 tbsp caster sugar

hefty pinch of salt

200ml (7fl oz) warm water

50ml (2fl oz) milk

30g (1oz) unsalted butter, melted

1 large free-range egg

500g (1lb 2oz) plain flour, sifted, plus extra for dusting

cooking oil, for oiling

50g (1¾oz) clarified butter, for cooking

8 ripe bananas

397g can condensed milk, to serve

To make the dough, dissolve the sugar and salt in the warm water in a large bowl, then add the milk and melted butter.

In a separate small bowl, beat the egg lightly and then add it to the liquid. Add all the sifted flour, then mix well. Knead the dough by hand on a lightly floured work surface, or using an electric mixer fitted with a dough hook, for at least 15 minutes. It should be tacky but not sticking to your hand. Lightly oil a bowl (to ensure the dough doesn't stick to the bowl) and place the dough in it. Cover the dough with clingfilm so that it's in contact with the dough to prevent it forming a crust, and leave to rest for at least 30 minutes.

Lightly oil a clean work surface. Pluck a piece of dough roughly 90g (3¼oz) in weight and smooth it into a ball by pulling the dough around itself in a spherical shape – it shouldn't take longer than 30 seconds. The ball should be smooth and tight, and around the size of a golf ball. Tuck the rest of the dough in and pinch it together, then place the dough ball on an oiled baking sheet. You should be able to make 8 from the dough.

Flatten a dough ball into a rough circular shape and then gently lift the side closest to you and drag it towards you. Lift quickly but delicately and slap it back on to the work surface. The elasticity and stickiness of the dough means that it shouldn't rip too easily and it stretches the dough thinly as you drag it. Repeat this process until the dough is roughly 2–3mm (1/16–1/8 in) thick – the thinner the better, though remember you have to lift it into a pan. A few holes are fine. Alternatively, you can use a rolling pin.

Meanwhile, heat half the clarified butter in a large frying pan over a medium heat – the butter needs to be really hot in order to crisp the dough, but not burned. Carefully lift the dough into the pan – it should sizzle. Slice a banana directly on to the centre of the roti. Fold the dough into a rectangular shape, flipping the sides in towards the centre so that they overlap and seal, and then flip it, adding a little more clarified butter if needed. Fry for roughly 3 minutes on each side until it is golden brown and crispy on both sides. Repeat this process with the other rotis. To serve, chop each roti into 4 squares and place on a plate, then drizzle with condensed milk.

➤➤ OTHER IDEAS

Replace the banana with chopped-up pineapple (see page 118).

Drizzle with melted chocolate instead of condensed milk

Lemon grass is such a versatile ingredient, as it can be used for both savoury and sweet dishes. These pears are poached in lemon grass syrup so that the flesh is soft and yielding. They can be served either as a dessert with a dollop of vanilla ice cream, or you can chop the pear up and eat it with yogurt for a decadent breakfast.

POACHED PEARS IN LEMON GRASS SYRUP

SERVES 2

Peel the pears and leave whole, with a bit of stalk. Take a saucepan large enough to hold the 2 pears, add the honey, lemon juice, lemon grass, water and ginger and bring to a simmer on a medium heat. Add the pears and cook on a gentle heat at a simmer, without the lid, for 30 minutes, turning the pears once halfway through. Then insert a knife into a pear – it should be tender. If not, simmer for a little while longer.

Remove the pears, then turn the heat up to reduce the syrup by a third. Strain the syrup through a fine sieve into a bowl and leave to cool for 20 minutes. Put the pears back in and leave to cool completely.

To serve, place a pear on each plate and drizzle with a little of the syrup.

2 Conference pears

3 tbsp clear honey

juice of ½ lemon

2 lemon grass stalks, finely chopped

600ml (20fl oz/1 pint) water

1 thin slice of fresh root ginger, peeled

1 tbsp caster sugar

CHAPTER

FRIDGE & FREEZER

FRIDGE & FREEZER

The fridge and freezer sections of most Asian supermarkets are not like those of their Western counterparts. In addition to basic raw ingredients, as you would expect to find in the West, they stock items that most people don't have the time or the expertise to make from scratch at home. I've included interesting cuts of meat that you usually come across in Asian supermarkets and indeed on restaurant menus, but I've given alternatives in case you find them too challenging to bear.

(1) TOFU (BEAN CURD)

Fresh forms of tofu are a big part of Asian cuisines. Besides the marinated, egg (*see page 135*) or deep-fried versions (tofu puffs), these are sold in tubs in water to keep them fresh. They range from extra-soft silken tofu, generally used for soups and sauces, to extra-firm tofu, which has the structure to stand up to stir-frying. Dispel any previously formed ideas (if you had them) that tofu is vegetarian food, used to replace meat, because it isn't so – it's a texture in its own right with a delicate flavour and often cooked with meat.

(2 & 3) DUMPLING WRAPPERS (SKINS)

While you can make your own potsticker wrappers (2), which are of a better quality than shop-bought, the ones you can buy in the fridge or freezer are still worth pursuing if you're short on time and/or energy. Wonton wrappers (3), however, are best left to the professionals and these can be purchased either ready to use from the fridge or ready to defrost from the freezer.

(4) KIMCHI

Kimchi is from Korea and hundreds of different versions are available. This is a method of preserving vegetables, and although the most common is made with cabbage, you can apply the kimchi treatment to almost any vegetable. The classic, Chinese cabbage (Chinese leaf or Napa cabbage), is rubbed with a glutinous rice flour paste to encourage fermentation, along with an eye-widening amount of chilli powder, garlic and other bits and bobs. Very traditional recipes use raw oysters in the mix too, which, given how long this stuff can sit in your fridge for, is frankly terrifying. Deliciously terrifying. Most Asian supermarkets will have at least the cabbage style in the fridge; for the more adventurous types, I've included a recipe to make your own at home – *see page 143*.

1.

4.

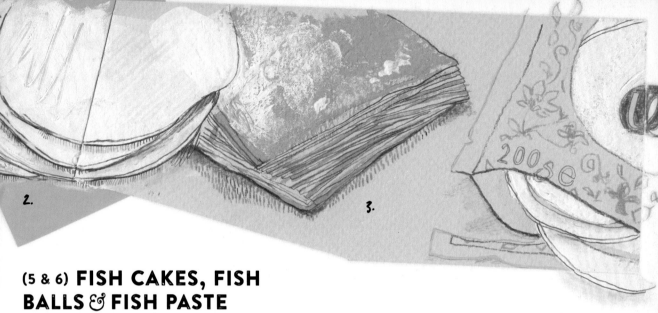

2.

3.

(5 & 6) FISH CAKES, FISH BALLS & FISH PASTE

Japanese fish cakes, called kamaboko, are a riot of colours and shapes. Some are decorated as cartoon characters, while others include pink swirls and other-worldly colours one might not be so used to eating. In most Asian supermarkets, the kinds of fish cakes (5) and balls (6) on offer are far more restrained and usually limited in range to different flavourings and preparation; some are fried before being packaged, others simply steamed. You can also buy the fish paste itself to shape whichever way you choose, usually found in the fridge or freezer. I've tried (several times) making my own fish balls at home, but they are just not as good as shop bought. It's something to do with the type of fish that's used that isn't available in the West; there's a certain kind of protein in this particular fish that when you break the flesh down and pound it repeatedly, it makes that characteristic bouncy texture. I always have a packet in the fridge to add to stir-fried dishes or noodle soups.

OFFAL

There's no denying it – Asians are probably among the more adventurous of the palate. In fact, they redefine nose-to-tail eating. I remember the haunted look in my friend's eye, followed by a shiver, as he recounted his holiday to Japan, during which he was served cod's sperm. I won't inflict bodily fluids on you, but chicken's feet, tendon and tripe are all worth trying.

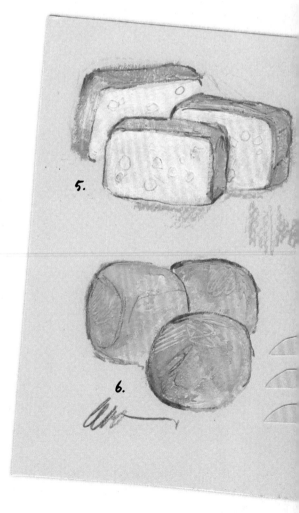

5.

6.

The classic Cantonese wonton contains pork and prawn, which makes it lighter; perfect for bobbing around in a noodle soup. This Sichuanese version is meatier and a little denser to stand up to the wallop of the spicy, lip-tingling chilli dressing.

SICHUAN WONTONS

For the wontons:

4 dried shiitake mushrooms, soaked in just-boiled water for 30 minutes, then drained and stems discarded

450g (1lb) minced pork – you want a bit of fat in this, so ask your butcher for it

100g (3½oz) soft silken tofu, drained well

1 tsp peeled and grated fresh root ginger

3 spring onions, very finely chopped

½ tsp ground white pepper

1 tsp sesame oil

1 tsp oyster sauce

½ tsp salt

1 packet fresh wonton wrappers / skins (leave them covered with a damp tea towel to prevent drying out when not in use)

plain flour, for dusting

For the sauce:

6 tbsp chilli oil with sediment (*see page 12*)

4 tbsp light soy sauce

1 tbsp Chinkiang black vinegar

1 tsp sesame oil

2 tsp sugar

2 tsp very finely chopped garlic

1 spring onion, diagonally sliced, to garnish

1. For the wontons, chop the mushrooms finely and mix with the pork in a large bowl. Break the tofu into chunks and add to the pork. Add all the other ingredients, except the wrappers and flour, and stir thoroughly with chopsticks until they have all combined well.

Take a wonton wrapper in your hand and place a corner pointing to your wrist. Add a scant tablespoon of filling to the centre.

Wet the top left- and right-hand edges with a finger dipped in water.

Bring the bottom edges up to meet the wet edges, and press to make a triangle.

Bring the bottom 2 points to meet around the front, wetting one edge to seal it.

Gently squeeze the air out of the area around the filling and seal well.

Place on a floured plate and repeat until all the filling is used up. Leftover wrappers should be wrapped well and frozen.

You can freeze the wontons on a floured baking sheet and combine in a freezer bag once frozen, then cook from frozen. Cook in a large saucepan of gently simmering water for 5–6 minutes (or 10 minutes if cooking from frozen) until they bob to the surface and are cooked through.

To make the sauce, combine the chilli oil, soy sauce, vinegar, sesame oil and sugar in a bowl. Mix well until all is incorporated, then stir in the garlic.

When the wontons are cooked, drain them well and combine with the sauce. Scatter the sliced spring onion on top as a garnish.

For a lighter, more summery dumpling filling, I like to use a higher ratio of prawn to pork. You still need the pork in there for juiciness and flavour, but this becomes more of a background binder. You can use any spring green vegetable: broad beans, watercress, peas... If you are using any vegetables that might give off moisture when cooked such as watercress or spinach, give them a quick blanch and squeeze dry before adding them to the mix.

PRAWN, ASPARAGUS & WILD GARLIC POTSTICKERS

MAKES AROUND
18

150g (5½oz) uncooked peeled prawns

1 tbsp bicarbonate of soda mixed with **2 tbsp** cold water (optional)

100g (3½oz) fatty minced pork

3 spring onions, finely sliced

1½ tsp peeled and very finely chopped fresh root ginger

1 tbsp light soy sauce

½ tsp salt

½ tsp sesame oil

pinch of ground white pepper

125g (4½oz) asparagus spears, trimmed of woody ends

50g (1¾oz) wild garlic leaves

1 tsp cornflour, plus **1 tsp** mixed with **2 tsp** cold water

1 packet round white dumpling wrappers / skins / gyoza (leave them covered with a damp tea towel to prevent drying out when not in use)

plain flour, for dusting

2 tbsp vegetable oil, plus a little extra for frying a sample of the filling to check the seasoning

For the dipping sauce:
3 tbsp Chinkiang black vinegar, or if you can't find it,

2 tbsp balsamic vinegar with **1 tsp** sherry vinegar

2.5cm (1in) piece of fresh root ginger, peeled and cut into fine julienne

1 red chilli, finely chopped (optional) – reserve half for garnish

This part is optional, but it makes the prawns extra juicy with an almost-crunchy texture: chop the prawns roughly and leave to marinate in the bicarbonate of soda solution while you prepare your other ingredients.

Add the pork, spring onions, ginger, soy sauce, salt, sesame oil and the white pepper to a large mixing bowl. Slice the asparagus spears into 1cm (½in)-thick rounds, reserving the tips for garnish, and finely chop the wild garlic, then add both to the bowl. Drain the prawns, pat dry with kitchen paper and add to the pork mixture. Use your hands to really get in there and make sure all the ingredients are mixed well and evenly distributed. Finally, add the dry cornflour and mix briefly again.

At this point, it's a good idea to fry a tablespoon of the pork mixture in a little vegetable oil in a nonstick frying pan and taste to check the seasoning.

Take a dumpling wrapper in your hand and add a tablespoon of the filling to the centre. Wet the edge of one half of the wrapper with a little of the cornflour paste to help it stick.

Fold the wrapper in half over the filling, pinching to seal the centre point.

Fold 3 pleats in each half to enclose the filling in the pouch: use your middle finger to bring the pastry round, with your thumb behind, to form the pleat.

05 Place on a floured plate, bottom down, so that they get a flat base. Repeat until all the filling is used up. (Leftover wrappers should be wrapped well and frozen.) At this point you can freeze the dumplings on a floured baking tray (provided your prawns or meat were not previously frozen), then once frozen, collect into a freezer bag. Cook from frozen (don't defrost them first.)

If cooking immediately, set a non-stick frying pan over a medium heat with the vegetable oil. Add the dumplings carefully to the oil and fry for about 3 minutes until the bottoms have browned. Add a few splashes of water and put a lid on so that the tops of the dumplings steam. The water may evaporate – if so, add a splash more so that you've steamed them for 5 minutes. Remove the lid; there shouldn't be much water left at this point; if there is, cook with the lid off until it has evaporated, and add a dribble of oil. Check the bottoms, they should be nicely bronzed.

Meanwhile, combine the dipping sauce ingredients in a small dish and serve on a platter, garnished with the asparagus tips, sliced in half and scattered, with the reserved red chilli sprinkled on top, if using. Serve the dumplings on a plate, upended to show off their lovely bronzed bottoms.

Give it a squeeze at the end to ensure it is sealed. Alternatively, bring the other half of the wrapper up to meet the wettened half and use the tines of a fork to seal, pressing any air out.

When I was a kid, I would make these with my mum and sister, a little production line of wrapping and folding, until we had hundreds of dumplings. Wontons are incredibly versatile; you can fill them with almost anything, as long as it doesn't release too much water. There are many ways of folding dumplings, but the one I've detailed here is the simplest.

CLASSIC DEEP-FRIED WONTONS

100g (3½oz) fatty minced pork

70g (2½oz) raw peeled prawns, roughly chopped

2 spring onions, finely chopped

3–4 dried shiitake mushrooms, soaked in just-boiled water for 30 minutes and then drained and diced, stems discarded

2.5cm (1in) piece of fresh root ginger, peeled and finely chopped

1½ tbsp oyster sauce

large pinch of ground white pepper

1 tsp light soy sauce

1 tbsp cornflour

1 packet fresh wonton wrappers / skins (leave them covered with a damp tea towel to prevent drying out when not in use)

plain flour, for dusting

vegetable oil, for deep-frying (optional)

Mix all the ingredients, except the wrappers, flour and oil, together thoroughly in a bowl. Leave it to sit for about 15 minutes.

Take a wonton wrapper in your hand and place a corner pointing to your wrist. Add a scant tablespoon of filling to the centre. Wet the top left- and right-hand edges with a finger dipped in water. Bring the bottom edges up to meet the wet edges, and press to make a triangle. Gently squeeze the air out of the area around the filling and seal well. Bring the bottom 2 points to meet around the front, wetting one edge to seal it. Place on a floured plate and repeat until all the filling is used up. Leftover wrappers should be wrapped well and frozen.

To cook, simmer gently in a large saucepan of water for 5–6 minutes (or 10 minutes if using from frozen) until they rise to the surface and are cooked through. If serving in a soup, don't cook them in soup stock, as the flour dusting on the wrappers will make it cloudy. Drain from the water and add to stock with or without noodles.

Alternatively, heat up enough oil to cover the wontons in a wok or large saucepan to 180°C (350°F), or until bubbles appear up the sides of a wooden chopstick when inserted into the hot oil. Fry, in batches, for 4–5 minutes. Remove and drain on kitchen paper, then serve with sweet chilli sauce.

Egg tofu is a type of flavoured silken tofu usually sold in tubes. It's made by adding eggs to the soya milk before the coagulant is added, and the whole lot is then cooked together so that the egg flavour is incorporated and the tofu takes on a yellow colour. Because it's incredibly delicate in texture, care must be taken when handling it. This tofu works really well dusted with flour and fried, and also braised afterwards, especially if you have issues with soft tofu's gelatinous texture. I particularly love the way the crispy crust becomes softer under the sauce of this dish, while retaining a little texture contrast.

BRAISED EGG TOFU *with* PORK *and* AUBERGINE

SERVES 4

3 tbsp cooking oil

2 slim Asian aubergines or 1 medium European aubergine, diced into large cubes

1 small tube of egg tofu

5 tbsp cornflour, for dusting

3 garlic cloves, very finely chopped

1 tsp peeled and very finely chopped fresh ginger

1 large red chilli, sliced into thin rounds

100g (3½oz) minced pork

400ml (14fl oz) chicken stock

2 tbsp oyster sauce

1 tbsp light soy sauce

1 tsp dark soy sauce

1 tsp sugar

1 tsp Chinkiang black vinegar

1 spring onion, thinly sliced into rounds, white and green parts separated

1 tsp cornflour, mixed with **1 tbsp** cold water

few sprigs of fresh coriander, to garnish

Heat up 1 tablespoon of the oil in a wok or a nonstick frying pan over a high heat and stir-fry the cubes of aubergine for 3–5 minutes so that the cubes take on some colour and become golden. Remove and place on a plate lined with kitchen paper.

Slice through the tube of the egg tofu in the centre with a sharp knife. Gently coax the egg tofu cylinders out of the plastic carefully on to a separate plate. Slice into rounds as thick as your forefinger, then pat dry with kitchen paper. Heat another tablespoon of oil in the frying pan over a medium heat, dust each round of egg tofu in cornflour and place in the oil. Fry for 3 minutes on a medium heat until one side has taken on a golden brown colour, then flip and repeat. Remove and place on another plate lined with kitchen paper. Repeat with the rest of the egg tofu rounds.

Heat up the last tablespoon of oil in a large saucepan, clay pot (*see page 11*) or wok over a medium heat and fry the garlic, ginger and chilli for 30 seconds or so until fragrant. Add the pork and stir-fry, amalgamating the garlic, ginger and chilli as you go, until the pork has taken on some golden colour. Put the aubergine back in, stir to combine, then add the stock, oyster sauce, soy sauces and sugar. Stir again to combine, then stir in the black vinegar. Add the tofu on top and carefully mix with a spoon so that the rounds drop into the liquid – it's OK if they aren't completely submerged.

Add the lid and braise for 5 minutes, then give it another gentle stir and braise for a further 5 minutes. Throw in the whites of the spring onion and the slaked cornflour and simmer for a couple of minutes to thicken. If using a clay pot, serve at the table, otherwise spoon out into a warmed serving bowl and garnish with the coriander and the spring onion greens. Serve with rice.

➥ OTHER IDEAS

Steam egg tofu with chopped-up prawns, chicken and a little soy sauce, or dip in tempura batter, deep-fry and serve with a sweet chilli dip.

Soft tofu is almost jelly-like in texture – you have to be quite careful with it so that it doesn't disintegrate on contact with your hands. This has been likened to a savoury panna cotta – you can dress firmer tofu with this spicy and tangy dressing, but I love the smooth, silky texture contrast with the crunchy peanuts.

STEAMED TOFU *with* SOY, SPRING ONION & CHILLI

SERVES 4 AS A SIDE DISH

Drain the tofu and carefully place it on a plate. Steam in a metal or bamboo steamer over a medium heat for 15 minutes.

Meanwhile, heat the cooking oil in a wok and fry the garlic for 30 seconds on a low heat, taking care not to burn it. Drain the garlic and place in a bowl.

Combine the soy sauces with the vinegar, sugar, chilli oil, oyster sauce and water and mix well, then carefully pour over the freshly steamed tofu. Garnish with the preserved vegetable, coriander, spring onion, Sichuan pepper and peanuts, and serve with rice while warm.

1 pack (300g or 340g) soft (not extra-soft) silken tofu (bean curd)

1 tbsp cooking oil

2 garlic cloves, very finely chopped

2 tbsp light soy sauce

½ tsp dark soy sauce

1 tsp Chinkiang black vinegar

1 tsp caster sugar

3 tbsp chilli oil (2 of the oil, 1 with sediment – *see page 12*)

1½ tbsp oyster sauce

1 tsp water

2 tsp Tianjin preserved vegetable (*see page 162*), well rinsed

small handful of fresh coriander, roughly chopped

1 spring onion, thinly sliced diagonally

½ tsp Sichuan peppercorns, toasted and finely ground

2 tbsp unsalted roasted peanuts, roughly chopped

The combination of salt, pepper(s), sugar and chilli makes an addictive, crisp coating for the tofu cubes, yielding to the soft, silky insides. Perfect as a snack with beer, or a side. This coating works perfectly with squid too – just cut the squid into rings and fry for a shorter length of time, just a minute or two.

SALT *and* PEPPER TOFU

1 block (about 340g / 11¾oz) firm tofu

cooking oil, for deep-frying

cornflour, for dusting

1 tsp ground white pepper

½ tsp Sichuan peppercorns, toasted and finely ground

1 tsp sugar

1 tsp salt flakes

3 garlic cloves, very finely chopped

3 large chillies, red and green, thinly sliced into rings – use bird's eye chillies if you prefer them hotter

2 large spring onions, halved lengthways and sliced into 2.5cm (1in) pieces

few sprigs of fresh coriander

wedge of lime

Pat the tofu dry with kitchen paper, then cut into 1cm (½in) cubes.

Pour 4cm (1½in) oil into a wok or saucepan and heat over a high heat to 180°C (350°F), or until bubbles appear up the sides of a wooden chopstick when inserted into the hot oil. Dust the tofu cubes in the cornflour, then slip into the oil, 5 or 6 at a time. Gently stir them with chopsticks or a metal spatula to prevent them from sticking. They should be crisp and golden after about 5 minutes. Remove with a slotted spoon and drain on kitchen paper. Return the oil to temperature before frying another batch.

While the tofu is frying, mix the 2 peppers, sugar and salt together in a small bowl.

When all the tofu cubes have been deep-fried and left to drain, pour off all but 2 tablespoons of the oil from the pan. Reheat the pan over a high heat. Add the garlic, chilli rings and spring onions and stir-fry for about 15 seconds until fragrant.

Add the tofu and sprinkle in the ground seasonings as you are cooking it. Cook for 1–2 minutes until golden, stirring constantly to allow the tofu to absorb the flavours. Transfer the tofu, along with all the bits in the pan, to a plate. Serve immediately, garnished with a few coriander sprigs and a lime wedge.

This is my take on a traditional Malaysian rojak salad. The amount of fruit in the salad as a savoury dish might make you suspicious, but the peanut and shrimp paste sauce balances out the sweet aspect. Deep-fried tofu puffs are excellent here; they soak up the sauce nicely and are a wonderfully soft texture against the crunch of the vegetables and fruit. Hae ko is yet another shrimp paste, made with sugar, but this type is essential in dishes like this, and also in the famous Penang assam laksa, a hot and sour fish soup. Serve with wooden skewers for people to stab at the salad, in traditional hawker style.

SPICY PEANUT and TOFU PUFF SALAD

SERVES **6** AS A SIDE, STARTER OR SNACK

Juice the limes into a bowl and add the red onion. This should cover the pieces, but if not, top up with a little water. Leave for 30 minutes.

Using 2 Chinese spoons stacked with a tofu puff in between, squeeze the excess water out of them. Chop into quarters and add to a large bowl. Add the pear, pineapple, cucumber, apple, mooli and bean sprouts.

Bash up the peanuts using a pestle and mortar so that they are quite fine, then remove from the mortar and set aside. Add the hae ko shrimp paste with the sugar, peanut butter and sriracha to the mortar and give the ingredients a few bashes so that they are all incorporated. The mixture will be very sticky at this point, so keep working it. Add the tamarind purée and soy sauce and mix well – really get in there and give it a good stir, as it'll be quite thick.

Drain the red onion and give the pieces a rinse, then drain again. Add to the salad, then pour all the dressing in. Mix really well – this may take 5 minutes of tossing and mixing. Sprinkle the crushed peanuts on top and give it another stir, then serve immediately.

2 limes

1 small red onion, roughly chopped

6 tofu puffs (*see page 128*), soaked in just-boiled water for 10 minutes, then drained

1 Asian pear, cored and chopped into bite-sized chunks

½ pineapple, peeled, cored and cut into bite-sized chunks (*see page 118*)

½ cucumber, deseeded and chopped into chunks

1 Granny Smith apple, cored and chopped into bite-sized chunks

50g (1¾oz) mooli (daikon), peeled and chopped into small chunks

large handful of bean sprouts, blanched in boiling water for 30 seconds, then drained

100g (3½oz) unsalted peanuts, toasted

2 tbsp hae ko (also called petis udang – *see page 17*)

2 tbsp palm sugar

1 tbsp smooth peanut butter

1 tbsp sriracha (*see page 109 for homemade, or use shop-bought*)

½ tbsp tamarind purée

2 tbsp light soy sauce

Marinated tofu is usually found in the fridge section of the Asian supermarket, and it takes the hassle out of you having to flavour tofu yourself. Invariably marinated in five-spice powder or chilli and sesame, it's the ideal weeknight staple for a stir-fried dish, and you can rustle this one up in under half an hour. It's bright and perky, and leftovers are also great cold as a salad. You can vary the vegetables, but to keep it visually interesting, try to get a good mix of colours and cut everything to the same sort of shape.

MARINATED TOFU & FIVE VEGETABLE STIR-FRY

SERVES 2

1 tbsp cooking oil

2.5cm (1in) piece of fresh root ginger, peeled and finely chopped

2 garlic cloves, very finely chopped

1 small carrot, sliced into 4cm (1½in) sticks

1 small courgette, sliced into 4cm (1½in) sticks

handful of green or purple kale, roughly chopped

2 purple cabbage leaves, finely sliced

100g (3½oz) marinated tofu (bean curd), chopped into bite-sized pieces

1 spring onion, white parts cut into 3cm (1¼in) lengths, green parts finely sliced into rings

50g (1¾oz) fine green beans or sugar snap peas

2 tbsp light soy sauce

handful of fresh coriander, roughly chopped

Heat your wok with the oil over a medium heat and swirl it around the edges to coat. Fry the ginger and garlic for 30 seconds, then add the carrot and courgette and stir-fry for 2–3 minutes until they start to become tender. Turn the heat up to high and add the kale and the purple cabbage. Add a splash of water and stir-fry the vegetables until the water has evaporated off, then add the tofu and another splash of water, and stir-fry again. Add the whites of the spring onion and the green beans or sugar snap peas and repeat the stir-frying process with another splash of water. Add the soy sauce and stir to combine, then add the spring onion greens and coriander and take the pan off the heat.

Serve with rice, or add cooked rice vermicelli noodles just after the green beans or sugar snap peas with the soy sauce for a noodle dish.

This stuff is dangerous. The first time I made it, I excitedly got the jar out of the cupboard to give it its first taste test. There were bubbles going up the side of the jar and a light fizzing noise could be heard emanating from it. I released the latch of the Kilner jar and it exploded up the wall. My housemate screamed. My kitchen smelled of fermented cabbage for a week. So don't overfill the Kilner jar; just use a second jar. Some people add raw oysters or salted shrimp to kimchi, but I'm too much of a wuss. Next time, next time...

MAKES

1–2 JARS

CABBAGE KIMCHI

Chop your Chinese cabbage up into even-sized pieces. Wash thoroughly, then coat liberally in salt, place in a colander and leave over a bowl or the sink for 3 hours, turning every 30 minutes or so. This is so that the salt leaches the moisture from the cabbage.

Whisk the water and the glutinous rice flour together in a saucepan and bring slowly to the boil, stirring all the time. Cook for a few minutes, then take off the heat. Leave to cool.

Stir in the chilli powder, then add the garlic, onion, ginger and apple. Add the fish sauce and mix well.

Wash the cabbage thoroughly, at least a few times to make sure all the salt has washed off. Drain well, put in a large bowl and toss in the spring onions, then add the chilli sludge. Combine well using your hands – if you have any cuts on your hands, wear gloves or it will sting.

Pack into a sterilized jar, leaving plenty of room from the top of the kimchi to the rim to allow for fermentation gases. Leave out on the side for a day or two, opening the lid every so often to let the gas escape, then transfer to the fridge. It's good to eat just as it comes for at least 3 weeks; after that it may become quite strong, but it's still fine to use in stews, stir-fries and other hot dishes.

2 heads of Chinese cabbage (Chinese leaf or Napa cabbage)

loads of table salt

250ml (9fl oz) water

60g (2¼oz) glutinous rice flour

110g (4oz) coarse Korean chilli powder

6 garlic cloves, very finely chopped

1 large onion, very finely chopped

5cm (2in) piece of fresh root ginger, peeled and grated

2 dessert apples, peeled, cored and grated

125ml (4fl oz) fish sauce

bunch of spring onions, chopped into thirds

Bread and cheese doesn't sound very Asian, but really, when you think about it, it makes sense. Kimchi is basically a pickle, and what goes better in a toasted cheese sandwich? Yup. Pickle. Strangely, the stronger cheeses work well with this; one might think they would clash, but actually the robust flavours meld together well.

KIMCHI TOASTED CHEESE SANDWICH

MAKES 1

Butter both sides of one slice of bread and place in a nonstick frying pan to assemble. Pile with half the cheese, then drape kimchi on top, pile on the rest of the cheese and carefully press the other slice of bread on top. Butter the exposed side of the top slice.

Heat the pan up gently to a medium heat and place a heavy heatproof object or pan on top of the sandwich to press it down. Add the cooking oil to the pan to help the browning along a bit. When the cheese on the bottom half looks like it's good and melted, check the underside for browning – it should be a deep golden. Flip the sandwich carefully, then place the heavy object or pan on top of the other side and cook for a further 5 minutes, checking a few times until the other underside is browned.

Take off the heat, slice the sandwich in half and wait a few minutes before devouring, as the cheese has a tendency to turn into molten lava.

spreadable butter

2 slices of sturdy bread, such as sourdough

handful of coarsely grated mature Cheddar cheese, or a 50/50 mix of Cheddar and Stilton

2 tbsp Cabbage Kimchi *(see page 143 for homemade)*, drained of juice and patted dry with kitchen paper

1 tsp cooking oil

This recipe uses slightly older kimchi – so, kimchi that's sat in the fridge for a while, to get a stronger flavour. If you have bought or made it fresh though, it will still work – just add a little more. This stew is so comforting that in colder weather I eat it at least once a week. The soft tofu is almost panna cotta-like in texture, while the egg, having poached in the broth, enriches it and makes it filling, like a big spicy hug.

KIMCHI STEW

SERVES 1

To make the broth, heat the water with the kombu and dried anchovies added until it is simmering. Take off the heat and add the bonito flakes. Leave for 15 minutes, then strain.

Heat the sesame oil in a dolsot (stone bowl – see page 11) or a saucepan and fry the garlic in the oil for a few minutes. Add the gochujang, the fresh chilli, if using, and the kimchi, then add the dashi broth and soy sauce. Simmer for 25 minutes, then add the tofu and simmer for a further 5 minutes. Break the egg into the stew and simmer for a further 3 minutes – if you're using a clay pot you can take this off the heat immediately and the egg will cook in the residual heat. Top with the spring onion, then transfer to a chopping board or heatproof mat. Serve with a bowl of steamed rice.

1 tsp sesame oil

1 tsp very finely chopped garlic

2 tsp gochujang (see page 16)

1 small red chilli, finely chopped (optional; add if you're a chilli head)

3 tbsp Cabbage Kimchi (see page 143 for homemade), plus 1 tbsp kimchi juice

1 tsp light soy sauce

200g (7oz) soft silken tofu (bean curd), drained, patted dry with kitchen paper

1 free-range egg

1 spring onion, finely sliced diagonally

For the broth:
300ml (10fl oz/½ pint) water

7.5cm (3in) square of dried kombu (see page 100)

4 dried anchovies, heads removed

small handful of dried bonito flakes (see page 209)

(or substitute all the above with **300ml /10fl oz / ½ pint** ready-made dashi stock)

This is one of those classic Chinese takeaway dishes, usually ordered with a load of spring rolls and some sweet and sour pork balls for a calorific and grease-laden start to a meal. It doesn't have to be though; while most takeaways deep-fry it, you can also shallow-fry it to retain some semblance of healthiness. The big bags of uncooked prawns you can buy at the supermarket are perfect for this, as you just need prawn meat and no shell.

SESAME PRAWN TOASTS

Using a rolling pin, roll the slices of bread to flatten them to half their width.

Pulse the prawns in a food processor with the spring onion, coriander, ginger, cornflour, soy sauce, white pepper and salt until you have a coarse paste. Stir in the water chestnut pieces.

Smear the prawn mixture on one side of the bread slices. Spread the sesame seeds out on a plate and dip the prawn side of the bread down on to them, pressing gently to make the seeds stick.

Heat up the cooking oil in a nonstick frying pan over a medium heat. Add the bread slices, sesame seed side down, and fry for 2–3 minutes, taking care that the seeds aren't burning. Flip over carefully and fry for a further 2–3 minutes until browned and crisp.

Drain on a piece of kitchen paper, then cut each slice into 4 pieces and serve with sriracha (*see page 109 for homemade, or use shop-bought*) or sweet chilli dipping sauce.

2–3 slices of stale white bread

150g (5½oz) uncooked peeled prawns, defrosted if frozen

1 spring onion, finely chopped

2 sprigs of fresh coriander, finely chopped

2.5cm (1in) piece of fresh root ginger, peeled and very finely chopped

1 tsp cornflour

1 tsp light soy sauce

pinch of ground white pepper

pinch of salt

3 drained canned water chestnuts, finely diced

4 tbsp white sesame seeds

50ml (2fl oz) cooking oil

Thai holy basil differs from its Italian counterpart in that the leaves are sturdier and tinged with purple. Flavour-wise, Italian (or sweet) basil is sweeter and milder, while Thai basil has a stronger aniseed note. Either can be used in this dish, though you should up the quantity of Italian basil for a stronger flavour.

PRAWNS *with* THAI BASIL

2 tbsp fish sauce
1 tbsp oyster sauce
1 tsp sugar
pinch of ground white pepper
1 tbsp cooking oil
8 garlic cloves, very finely chopped
1 large red chilli, thickly sliced into rings
1 small white onion, thinly sliced into half-moons
50g (1¾oz) sugar snap peas or mangetout, cut in half
10 uncooked peeled king prawns
2 small ripe tomatoes, quartered
small handful of Thai basil, or a hefty handful of Italian basil, leaves plucked from the stems
juice of ½ lime

Combine the fish sauce, oyster sauce, sugar and white pepper with 1 tablespoon water in a bowl.

Heat the oil in a wok on a medium heat, add the garlic and fry gently for 3–4 minutes, then add the chilli and stir to combine.

Add the half-moons of onion, then turn the heat up to high and stir-fry for 1 minute, making sure that the garlic doesn't catch. Add the sugar snap peas or mangetout and 3 tablespoons of water, then stir-fry continuously until the water has evaporated. Still on the highest heat, add the prawns and stir-fry for 1 minute. Then add the tomatoes, basil and the sauce ingredients, and stir-fry continuously, shaking the pan once or twice, until the prawns have turned pink.

Take the pan off the heat and add the lime juice, then serve with rice or noodles.

Soft shell crabs are something of a rarity in normal supermarkets and fishmongers, but you can often find them in Asian supermarkets in the freezer section. They are best entombed in a carapace of batter for that crisp contrast to the softness of the crabmeat, and though they are not cheap, they make an impressive impact; almost prehistoric-looking in this burger. If you can't find them, then large uncooked peeled prawns are a great substitute. It's a messy business eating this thing, but then most burgers are.

MAKES
6
BURGERS

TEMPURA SOFT-SHELL CRAB BURGERS

Use shop-bought brioche buns if you can find them, or make your own as follows. These are also great with traditional beef burgers

For the buns:

40ml (1½fl oz) milk, warmed

300ml (10fl oz/½ pint) water

2½ tbsp sugar

7g sachet fast-action dried yeast

450g (1lb) strong white flour, plus extra for dusting

150g (5½oz) plain flour

1½ tsp salt

30g (1oz) butter, diced

1 free-range egg, beaten

1 free-range egg yolk beaten with **1 tbsp** milk, for glazing

white sesame seeds, for sprinkling

For the burgers:

175g (6oz) plain flour

2 tbsp cornflour

1 tsp salt

6 soft-shell crabs, defrosted overnight in the fridge, or **6** large uncooked prawns per person

600ml (20fl oz/1 pint) cooking oil

400ml (14fl oz) ice-cold sparkling water

For the accompaniments:

4 tbsp sriracha *(see page 109 for homemade, or use shop-bought)*, mixed well into **8 tbsp** mayonnaise and **1 tbsp** lemon juice

1 red onion, halved, sliced into thin rounds and soaked in cold water for 20 minutes

Pickled Mooli *(see page 157)* or shop-bought gherkins

4 Little Gem lettuce leaves, finely shredded

Tempura is a Japanese method of coating vegetables, meat or fish in a crisp, light and greaseless batter – the key to getting it right is making sure everything is as cold as you can get it, and that it's not left hanging around. Tempura waits for no one.

To make the buns, add the warm milk, water, sugar and yeast to a small bowl and give the ingredients a good mix. Meanwhile, add the 2 flours and salt to a separate bowl and rub in the butter to create a crumbly texture. Add the beaten whole egg, then mix in the yeast mixture. Combine well. Knead by hand on a lightly floured work surface, or using an electric mixer fitted with a dough hook, for 10 minutes until it's nice and smooth. Put it back into the bowl, cover it with clingfilm and leave to rise in a warm place for an hour until double the size.

Divide the dough into 6 and roll each into a large burger bun shape. Place on a baking sheet lined with greaseproof paper, leaving enough room between them for them to expand while cooking. Leave for an hour. Meanwhile, preheat your oven to 200°C (400°F) Gas Mark 6.

Glaze the buns with the egg yolk and milk mixture and sprinkle with sesame seeds. Place a tray of water on the bottom shelf of the oven, then bake the buns for 15 minutes on the middle shelf. Remove from the oven and leave to cool on a wire rack.

Preheat your oven to 110°C (225°F) Gas Mark ¼. For the tempura, sift the flour into a bowl with the cornflour and salt. Refrigerate the flour mixture for at least half an hour before you use it. Drain the defrosted soft-shell crabs and pat dry with kitchen paper. Pour the oil for deep-frying into a wok or large saucepan and heat to 190°C (375°F), or until a breadcrumb dropped in sizzles heartily. Just before you are due to use the flour mixture, add the sparkling water and mix briefly with chopsticks – it's OK if it's lumpy – then immediately coat each crab with the batter. Drop, one or two at a time, into the hot oil and fry for 4–6 minutes until browned and crisp. Remove and place on a wire rack in the preheated oven while you cook the rest.

To assemble, halve a burger bun and smear the sriracha mayonnaise on both cut sides of the bun halves. Place the half-moons of red onion, a couple slices of pickle and a little of the shredded lettuce on the base of the bun. Place the soft shell crab inside and top with the lid. You may need to squish the burger down a bit so that it all melds together properly. Do the same with the rest of the buns and crabs.

If you wanted to, you could grind your own spices and make a deep, rich, aromatic curry sauce for this, but that's not really in keeping with the nature of the dish. Bouncy fish balls in a sweet and mild curry sauce is how you find them in Hong Kong, or in dim sum steamer baskets. It is similar to the kind of chip-shop-curry-sauce flavour; a bit cheap, a bit addictive. In the summer time, you could do as the street food vendors of Hong Kong do – skewer fish balls (in this instance you would use normal white ones), give them a lick of oil and barbecue them until crisp and golden. A pot of this curry sauce is essential for dunking.

HONG KONG HAWKER-STYLE CURRY FISH BALLS

SERVES 6 AS A SNACK

Place the fish balls in a bowl and fill with just-boiled water. Soak for 10 minutes to get rid of the excess oil.

Heat the oil in a saucepan and fry the onion with the garlic over a medium heat until soft and translucent. Add the flour and stir well so that it is evenly coating the onion and garlic. Stir in the curry powder.

Add the water, bit by bit, whisking out any lumps that might develop. Stir in the coconut milk along with the salt and sugar.

Peel the mooli and roll cut it: hold the mooli in front of you and make the first cut with your knife at a 45° angle. Roll the vegetable 90° away from you and cut again, repeating until you get to the end. Add this to the pan and stir to combine. Partially cover and simmer gently for 40 minutes – by this time it should be thick and creamy. Add the ketchup and Worcestershire sauce and stir to combine.

Serve as a snack with cocktail sticks and napkins for everyone to pick at.

227g packet fried fish balls (*see page 129*)

1 tbsp cooking oil

½ onion, diced

3 garlic cloves, very finely chopped

2 tbsp plain flour

2 heaped tbsp medium curry powder

500ml (18fl oz) water

150ml (5fl oz/¼ pint) coconut milk

hefty pinch of salt

1 tsp sugar

200g (7oz) mooli (daikon)

1 tbsp tomato ketchup

splash of Worcestershire sauce

Although it looks deceptively simple with a clear broth and milky white colourings, this fish ball noodle soup is full of flavours of the sea from the dried seafood in the stock. I employ a traditional Vietnamese technique used for making pho by charring the onion, for an extra dimension of flavour.

FISH BALL NOODLE SOUP

SERVES 4

400g (14oz) dried rice vermicelli noodles, or fresh ho fun noodles

1 tsp sesame oil (if using fresh noodles)

1 onion, unpeeled, sliced into quarters

1 litre (1¾pints) water

2 tbsp dried anchovies, washed and the heads pinched off

1 tbsp dried shrimps, washed

1 thin slice of fresh root ginger, peeled

1 star anise

20g (¾oz) lard

4 red Asian shallots, very thinly sliced

16 fish balls (see page 129)

1 head of pak choi, sliced through the head into quarters

1 tbsp fish sauce

1 spring onion, green part only, finely sliced into rings

For dried noodles, soak in boiling water as per the packet instructions, then drain. For fresh ho fun noodles, soak in warm water until the strands have loosened, then simmer for a minute and drain. Run under cold water and toss with 1 tsp sesame oil.

Char the onion quarters over the flame of a gas hob or under the grill until browned and a little blackened on each side. Add to the water in a saucepan, along with the anchovies, shrimps, ginger and star anise. Simmer gently over a low heat for 40 minutes, then drain through a fine sieve into a new saucepan.

Meanwhile, put the lard into a small saucepan on a low heat until it has melted, then add the shallots and turn the heat up to medium. Stir them a couple of times and fry for 3–5 minutes until they are a light golden brown. Take the pan off the heat and remove the shallots with a slotted spoon to kitchen paper. Reserve the lard.

To assemble the dish, add the noodles to each bowl. Reheat the stock on a high heat so that it is boiling, add the fish balls and cook in the stock for 3 minutes. Add the pak choi, then turn the heat down to medium and cook for 1 minute. Take the pan off the heat and add the fish sauce.
Add a pak choi quarter and 4 fish balls to each bowl. Ladle stock into the bowl so that the noodles are in the soup but not drowning. Garnish with ½ tablespoon of the used lard, a teaspoon of the shallots and a quarter of the spring onion greens per bowl. Serve immediately.

Known as 'yong tau fou' you can use the fish paste to stuff a variety of vegetables – long, mild chillis, halved peppers and okra are popular. I particularly like using aubergine for the silkiness that the aubergine flesh takes on after having been fried and braised. It may have something to do with the aubergine being my favourite vegetable too. It's completely customizable, but the spring onion gives the fish paste a clean sprightliness, though you could experiment with a flavouring of fresh coriander, or even seaweed. Traditionally, these are deep-fried and then braised, but I've found that shallow-frying doesn't alter them detrimentally.

FISH PASTE-STUFFED AUBERGINE

SERVES 4 AS A SIDE DISH

Slice the aubergines widthways into thick slices, about 2 fingers wide. Then slice each section in half, not quite cutting all the way through. Place in a colander, sprinkle with the salt and leave over a bowl or the sink for 20 minutes.

Meanwhile, finely chop the spring onions. Mix with the fish paste and set aside.

Mix all the sauce ingredients together, except the cornflour solution. Prepare a plate with some cornflour on it for dusting the aubergine.

Rinse the aubergine and dry with kitchen paper. Using a tablespoon and your fingers, carefully stuff the fish paste down the slits of each aubergine segment, as much as the aubergine can take without breaking. Place the aubergine on the plate of cornflour, turn them so that they are evenly coated, dust off the excess and transfer to a clean plate. Repeat with the remaining aubergine slices.

Heat the oil up in a wok on a high heat until shimmering but not smoking. Reduce the heat to medium and cook the aubergine for 4 minutes on each side until browned and starting to soften. Add the sauce mixture, place the lid on and braise for 10 minutes.

Stir the cornflour solution into the wok and simmer for a minute until the sauce has thickened before serving.

2 slim Asian aubergines or
1 medium European aubergine
2 tbsp salt
2 spring onions
200g (7oz) fish paste (see page 129)
cornflour, for dusting
3 tbsp cooking oil

For the sauce:
1 tbsp light soy sauce
1½ tbsp oyster sauce
pinch of sugar
1 tbsp Shaoxing rice wine
200ml (7fl oz) chicken stock
1 tsp cornflour, mixed with
1 tbsp cold water

I grew up eating beef tendon, usually in anise-scented noodle soups, so the thought of it doesn't affect me much. It actually makes my mouth water a little. Technically classed as offal, it's not a usual sight at the butcher, but you will find it in the frozen section of the Asian supermarket. It needs to be cooked for a long time for the cartilage to break down to its gelatinous state. It's perfect in these buns – in a classic Cantonese-style sweet and sour sauce, the pickled mooli (daikon) and peanuts give a much-needed crunch. You can substitute crispy fried chicken or pork for the beef tendon if you can't find it.

SERVES 4

SWEET *and* SOUR BEEF TENDON *with* STEAMED BUNS

500g (1lb 2oz) beef tendon, defrosted if frozen

1 litre (1¾ pints) water

1 star anise

1 tbsp cooking oil

6 garlic cloves, very finely chopped

1 tsp very finely chopped fresh root ginger

150g (5½oz) pineapple flesh, cut into bite-sized chunks *(see page 118)*

For the sauce:

3 tbsp water

1 tbsp gochujang *(see page 16)*

2 tbsp tomato ketchup

2 tbsp orange juice

1½ tbsp cider vinegar

1 tbsp Worcestershire sauce

1 tbsp light soy sauce

2 tbsp sugar

To serve:

1 packet frozen mantou (steamed bread buns)

1 quantity Pickled Mooli *(see opposite)*

70g (2½oz) peanuts, toasted and ground to a coarse powder

large bunch of fresh coriander

Bring a large saucepan of water to the boil. Rinse the beef tendon and blanch in the boiling water for 3 minutes, then drain and rinse again. Return to the saucepan with the 1 litre (1¾ pints) water and the star anise and simmer on a gentle heat with the lid on for 3–4 hours until tender. Drain the tendon and leave to cool, then chop into largish bite-sized chunks.

While the tendon is cooling, mix all the sauce ingredients together.

Heat the oil in a wok on a medium-high heat. Add the garlic and ginger and stir-fry for about 20 seconds until just aromatic. Add the pineapple and the sauce mixture, and stir to coat. Let the sauce simmer for about 2 minutes to allow the pineapple to become tender. Return the beef tendon to the pan and toss until it is well coated with the sauce. Leave on a low heat to keep warm.

Steam the mantou buns according to the packet instructions. Slice each open, stuff with a piece of tendon, a chunk of pineapple and the pickled mooli and add a sprinkling of the coarse peanut powder. Garnish each with a sprig of coriander.

Mooli, or daikon or Asian radish, is a perfect pickling vegetable, as it's sturdy enough to cope with the treatment, but mild in flavour to go with many things. Eat this in banh mi-style sandwiches, on top of noodle soups, shredded in salads, or simply as a side with rich meat dishes.

PICKLED MOOLI

450g (1lb) mooli (daikon)
1 large red chilli (optional)
400ml (14fl oz) warm water
3 tbsp rice vinegar
5 tbsp white caster sugar
1 tbsp fine salt

MAKES
1 LARGE JAR

Peel the mooli and slice into rounds half as thick as a pound coin, then slice in half. Place in a clean, sterilized jar or container.

If using the chilli, break it in half and add this on top of the mooli. Mix the warm water with the vinegar, sugar and salt, and stir until everything is combined – the mixture should cover the pickles. Pour over the mooli in the jar. Add the lid and place in the fridge. Eat after a day – it will last up to a month in the fridge.

To the Chinese, chicken's feet are an everyday sight, common on dim sum and restaurant menus. As a child, I watched fascinated as my grandmother noisily sucked all the skin off the chicken's feet and spat the bones out delicately into a little pile on the table. The point of them is that skin and cartilage – a wonderful vehicle for this spicy, finger-licking sauce.

SERVES 6 AS A STARTER OR SIDE DISH

KOREAN-STYLE CHICKEN'S FEET

300ml (10fl oz/½ pint) vegetable oil, for deep-frying

300g (10½oz) chicken's feet, defrosted if frozen, toenails clipped off with kitchen scissors and very thoroughly dried

For the sauce:

1 tbsp sesame oil

1 small onion, diced

3 garlic cloves, very finely chopped

2.5cm (1in) piece of fresh root ginger, peeled and very finely chopped

3 tbsp gochujang (*see page 16*)

1 tbsp Korean chilli flakes

400ml (14fl oz) water

2 tbsp light soy sauce

1 tbsp dark soy sauce

1 tsp rice vinegar

3 tbsp sugar

Pour the oil for deep-frying into a wok or large saucepan and heat to 180°C (350°F), or until bubbles appear up the sides of a wooden chopstick when inserted into the hot oil. Deep-fry the chicken's feet for about 5–7 minutes until the skin has puffed up and browned slightly. Remove with a slotted spoon and leave to drain on a wire rack.

Heat the sesame oil in a saucepan on a medium heat and fry the onion, garlic and ginger for 5 minutes, stirring so that they don't brown. Add the gochujang, chilli flakes and the water and stir until thoroughly combined. Add the soy sauces, vinegar and sugar, followed by the chicken's feet. Braise on a low heat with the lid half off for 30 minutes, then turn all the chicken's feet around and braise for another 30 minutes. By this point the sauce should be reduced and sticky; if not, remove the chicken's feet and reduce the sauce down by simmering it until it becomes a sticky glaze, which could take anything from 10–20 minutes. Pour over the chicken's feet and serve with napkins for messy fingers.

OTHER IDEAS

Steam chicken's feet in black bean sauce, or braise Filipino style in 'adobo'.

Unlike pork belly or lamb shanks that have had a fairly recent resurgence in popularity, the same can't be said for poor old tripe. With granny's house whiffing of tripe boiled with onions being forever etched into the collective memory or simply squeamishness over eating a cow's stomach lining, it's difficult to convince people to give it a chance. The Chinese don't have such hang-ups, and it is prized for its texture. In fact, Asian and Caribbean butchers are the only place I've seen it for sale. This spicy, tangy, in-your-face preparation might go some way to helping you get over your fears.

FIVE-SPICE *and* CHILLI OIL COLD TRIPE SALAD

SERVES 4 AS A SNACK

Bring the tripe to the boil in a saucepan of water and boil for 3 minutes, then drain, rinse and pat dry with kitchen paper.

Heat the cooking oil in a large saucepan and fry the garlic and ginger on a medium heat until fragrant. Add the star anise, cinnamon stick and five-spice, and stir-fry briefly until fragrant. Add the mandarin peel, the tripe and the beef brisket and the water, then simmer over a very gentle heat for 2 hours. Leave to cool in the liquor.

Remove the brisket and tripe from the liquor (which can now be discarded) and slice both thinly. Add to a large bowl.

For the dressing, bash the garlic clove with the ginger using a pestle and mortar, then stir in the chilli oil, sesame oil, Sichuan pepper, black vinegar, sugar and salt. Taste the dressing; it should be salty, sweet, spicy and tangy in a good balance. Just before serving, stir in the coriander, then add the dressing to the brisket and tripe.

150g (5½oz) tripe
1 tbsp cooking oil
2 garlic cloves
1 slice of fresh root ginger, peeled
2 star anise
1 cinnamon stick
2 tsp five-spice powder
(*see page 205 for homemade*)
1 whole dried mandarin peel, soaked in just-boiled water for about 10 minutes until soft, then drained
150g (5½oz) beef brisket
500ml (17fl oz) water

For the dressing:
1 garlic clove, peeled
1 tsp peeled and grated fresh root ginger
3 tbsp chilli oil with sediment
(*see page 12*)
1 tbsp sesame oil
1 tsp Sichuan peppercorns, toasted and finely ground
1 tbsp Chinkiang black vinegar
1 tsp sugar
½ tsp salt
small handful of roughly chopped fresh coriander

PICKLES & PRESERVES

PICKLES & PRESERVES

I've always loved anything pickled or preserved, even as a child. As a precocious eight-year-old, I was found in the kitchen smearing butter on water crackers with my fingers and topping them with half a pitted black olive and a sliver of pickled onion. I still have a habit of eating cornichons straight from the jar, fishing the capers out of the brine, and often my favourite part of a burger is the gherkin. I love sour things, though my teeth hate me for it.

Most cultures and cuisines have a method of preserving food, from air-drying or smoking, to brining and salting. The Asian cultures are no different, and Asian supermarkets hold a vast treasure trove of pickled goods. I'm often found wandering the aisles, studying the limited English writing on the sides. Most often, I hoard serving-sized vacuum packets of various vegetables, sometimes with 'Nutrition for students' bafflingly printed on them. I can only assume it is in reference to their longevity. These are great as rice or congee toppings (*see page 58*). This is by no means an exhaustive list, but rather a guide to what I've found most readily available.

A lot of the preserved vegetables you'll find are mustard greens. They are sturdy vegetables, making them the ideal candidate for pickling. You can buy them in various guises, from their soft leaves to the vivid, angry-red bulbs of their stems. They can be found in liquid or dry packed in salt, canned or vacuum packed. Most, if not all, pickled and preserved vegetables should be washed beforehand to remove some of the excess salt and brine.

PICKLED MUSTARD GREEN

This is your standard head of mustard green, usually halved, in brine and vacuum packed. Some may have a lone red chilli floating in there with them. These are good all-rounders for soups and stir-fried dishes.

SICHUAN ZHA CAI

If you have wandered around any Chinese wet markets, you will have seen this bulbous livid-red thing in open-topped barrels. In supermarkets, they are most often found canned or shredded in a vacuum pack. This is the root of the mustard green, and it is salted and pressed before fermenting with chilli paste, a bit like kimchi (*see page 143*). You can stir-fry this with shredded pork, fold it into noodles or use it to top tofu (bean curd) or congee (*see page 58*) for a spicier pickle kick.

SICHUAN YA CAI

This consists of the leaves only of the mustard green, chopped up and left to ferment with salt, and they're essential in dishes like dan dan noodles and dry-fried green beans. I've only ever found these in vacuum-packed foil bags.

MUI CHOI

Again, this is another form of mustard green but instead of being pickled in brine, it's dried and packed in salt, sometimes with the addition of sugar. Due to the preservation process, you must rinse these thoroughly, otherwise your dish can become gritty. It is most often used in braised meat dishes.

OLIVE VEGETABLE

From southern China and a Teochew local delicacy, olive vegetable is a dark and murky paste that comes in a jar. It's actually the leaves of mustard greens mashed and preserved with black olive flesh and oil; sometimes you'll find olive stones in the jar. It's dramatically dark and great for stir-frying with – just hold off on the salt, as it's plenty salty enough as it is.

TIANJIN PRESERVED VEGETABLE

This is one of my favourite pickled vegetables. From the Tianjin metropolis of northern China, this is made with Chinese cabbage (Chinese leaf or Napa cabbage); the pieces of cabbage are sun-dried, then combined with salt and garlic before being placed in an earthenware pot to ferment. You usually buy it in clay pots, and it lasts forever in the cupboard. A quick rinse before using it is essential, as it's very salty.

KIMCHI

Often called the national dish of Korea, almost any vegetable can be given the kimchi treatment, 'kimchi' referring to the spicing and fermentation process (*see pages 48 and 143*).

DRIED LILY BUDS/FLOWERS

Also called golden needles, but not to be confused with golden needle mushrooms, these are the unopened flowers of day lilies. Sold in packets, they look like brown woody stems and need to be rehydrated in just-boiled water before using them. Some recipes call for them to be tied in knots before use to prevent them from breaking up. If you have nimble fingers, then crack on, otherwise it's not that critical if you don't knot them. The buds taste slightly floral and woody, but not overwhelming, and suit stir-fries and braises.

TSUKEMONO

This is the collective term for Japanese pickles. Most Japanese pickles are for eating with meals – accompaniments rather than for cooking with. Japanese sections will often have a variety of brightly coloured pickles, ranging from yellow to purple, and red to green. I use umeboshi plums most often, as a snack or a filling for onigiri (rice balls).

SOUR BAMBOO SHOOTS

Available in a jar preserved in brine or vacuum packed, sour bamboo shoots are mostly used in Thai cooking. They have a very distinctive aroma that will linger if you leave any open and hanging around. They are best suited to soups and curries – *see page 174*.

CENTURY EGGS

These are ready-to-eat duck eggs that have been buried in alkaline clay for some time so that when peeled the whites of the egg are black and transparent, and the yolks green-grey. Most people baulk when they see these, as they are certainly dramatic looking, but they are also mellow in flavour. Expensive premium century eggs have a still-runny yolk. Chop the eggs up into congee (*see page 58*) or soups, or stir-fry them with minced chicken, basil and chilli. They are also great in salads (*see page 176*).

SALTED EGGS

These are duck eggs that have been preserved by submerging them in brine or by packing a damp charcoal paste around them, often sold with the charcoal residue still in place. This preserving process renders the egg white very white and liquid, while the egg yolk takes on a firmer, slightly fudgy consistency. They are not immediately ready to eat; once cooked, they impart a great eggy saltiness and a sandy texture. The Chinese use salted egg yolks in not only savoury but sweet dishes, notably mooncakes eaten at Mid-autumn Festival; those made with the yolk are the most expensive, and the yolk is said to symbolize the moon. To use the yolk, crack the egg and discard the egg white. Otherwise, boil the egg as you would do a normal egg.

WHITE & RED FERMENTED TOFU (BEAN CURD)

Often called 'Chinese cheese', white fermented tofu is cured in brine to create funky, silky smooth cubes that are sold in jars. It's usually eaten as a condiment, as a rice or congee topping (*see page 58*) straight from the jar, but it's also stir-fried with vegetables (*see page 183*). It's available flavoured with sesame or chilli oil as well as plain. The red variety, available in jars or cans, is tofu that has been fermented in red rice yeast and is much stronger in taste. It's rarely eaten as it is but is used for marinating and braising meat.

Dill is a herb I associate with Scandinavian cuisine and, in turn, smoked salmon, mackerel and gravadlax. But it's used all over the world, from the Mediterranean, through the Middle East and even China. This broth-based soup is light, fragrant and flavoursome, with the hearty tang of the mustard green at the forefront.

VIETNAMESE PICKLED MUSTARD GREEN & MEATBALL SOUP

SERVES 4 AS A LIGHT LUNCH

350g (12oz) minced pork

2.5cm (1in) piece of fresh root ginger, peeled and finely chopped

1 garlic clove, very finely chopped

scant handful of fresh coriander, finely chopped

1 tbsp oyster sauce

½ tsp salt

pinch of ground white pepper

1 tsp cornflour

1 litre (1¾ pints) chicken stock

1 red bird's eye chilli, split in half (optional)

1 pickled mustard green (*see page 160*), drained and soaked in cold water for 30 minutes

pinch of sugar

2 large tomatoes, cut into 8 wedges

1 small bunch of dill, cut into 2.5cm (1in) segments

1–2 tbsp fish sauce

Combine the pork with the ginger, garlic, coriander, oyster sauce, salt, white pepper and cornflour in a bowl, mixing well with your hands so that the mixture holds together well, though don't over-mix, otherwise the meatballs will be tough. Form into golf ball-sized balls.

Heat the stock in a saucepan over a high heat until it's simmering, then lower the heat to avoid it boiling. Add the halved chilli, if using. Chop the mustard green into bite-sized pieces, discarding the tough stalk, drop it into the stock and simmer for 10 minutes. Add the meatballs, sugar, tomatoes and two-thirds of the dill and simmer for a further 15 minutes on a gentle heat. Add 1 tablespoon of fish sauce and taste, then add more if needed.

Add the rest of the dill, then serve.

This is the kind of home comfort meal I love most, one that I make when I'm eating alone and I don't have any guests to entertain, which seems silly since it's so quick and tasty. It's what I imagine my younger self might have lived off had I gone to university. The noodle sauce is spicy and tangy from the preserved vegetable; creamy and satisfying from the egg. The key to fluffy, soft eggs is for the egg mixture to hit hot, plentiful oil to allow it to bubble and fluff up.

SICHUAN PRESERVED VEGETABLE, EGG *and* TOMATO NOODLES

SERVES 2

Bring a saucepan of water to the boil to cook the noodles as per the packet instructions.

Meanwhile, heat 1 tablespoon of the cooking oil in a wok over a medium heat. Add the garlic, preserved vegetable and the whites of the spring onion and stir-fry for 2 minutes, then add the tomatoes and stir-fry for a minute or two until the tomatoes are starting to soften and release their juices. Add the water, sugar, ketchup, rice wine and soy sauce. Simmer for a minute, then remove to a bowl and wipe the wok clean.

Drain the noodles well and place in a large warmed dish.

Add the remaining 4 tablespoons of cooking oil to the wok, giving it a good swirl and heating it up over a medium to high heat until it's just below smoking.

Add the beaten eggs to the oil – they will puff up and sizzle. Stir the egg with chopsticks until it has scrambled a little, then add the cooked tomato mixture back in with the greens of the spring onion and stir and fold a couple of times. If the sauce is looking too watery, add the cornflour solution. If it's catching on the wok, add a splash more water.

Take the pan off the heat and pour the contents over the noodles, drizzling the chilli oil on top before serving.

200g (7oz) bundle of dried wide, flat wheat noodles

5 tbsp cooking oil

2 garlic cloves, very finely chopped

knob of Sichuan zha cai preserved vegetable (*see page 162*), soaked in water for 20 minutes, then rinsed and finely chopped

1 spring onion, white and green parts separated, finely chopped

2 large ripe tomatoes, roughly chopped

50ml (2fl oz) water

pinch of sugar

squeeze of tomato ketchup

1 tsp Shaoxing rice wine

1 tsp light soy sauce

2 free-range eggs, beaten with a pinch of salt

1 tsp cornflour, mixed with **1 tbsp** cold water (optional)

1 tsp chilli oil

Chinese sausage (lap cheong) works well in this dish due to its sweetness contrasting with the intensely savoury olive vegetable, which is like a Chinese tapenade *(see page 162)* that speckles everything dramatically with black. Watch out for olive stones.

OLIVE VEGETABLE FRIED RICE *with* CHINESE SAUSAGE

SERVES 4

3 tbsp cooking oil

2 Chinese sausages, diced

splash of Shaoxing rice wine

2.5cm (1in) piece of fresh root ginger, peeled and very finely chopped

2 garlic cloves, very finely chopped

1 carrot, peeled and diced

1 celery stick, peeled and diced

handful of sugar snap peas, chopped into thirds

350g (12oz) cooled cooked rice

1 tbsp light soy sauce

3 tbsp olive vegetable *(see page 162)*

1 spring onion, finely chopped

4 free-range eggs

sriracha *(see page 109 for homemade, or use shop-bought)*, to serve

Heat your wok with 2 tablespoons of the cooking oil. Just before it starts smoking, add the diced Chinese sausage and stir-fry for 1–2 minutes to release some of the oils. Splash the rice wine in and stir until it has evaporated. Add the ginger and garlic and stir-fry for 30 seconds, then add the carrot and celery, followed by the sugar snap peas. Stir-fry for 1 minute to soften the vegetables.

Over a high heat, add the rice by crumbling it through your fingers to make sure that the grains are separated. Leave the rice to fry until the grains near the centre of the wok start jumping, then start moving the rice around. Drizzle over the soy sauce and stir-fry again, then add the olive vegetable, moving the rice around constantly so that it distributes evenly. Stir in the spring onion and set the wok aside.

Heat up the remaining tablespoon of cooking oil in a nonstick frying pan and fry all 4 eggs for 3 minutes over a medium heat, then put the lid on and fry for 2 minutes more to ensure that the yolks are still runny but the whites have set.

To serve, spoon each serving of the rice into a bowl and upend on to a plate to create a dome shape. Drape a fried egg on top and serve with sriracha for people to help themselves.

➼ OTHER IDEAS

Braise cubes of butternut squash with olive vegetable made into a sauce with a little stock, or serve with congee *(see page 58)*.

There are two different types of mui choi, sweet and salty, and this recipe uses both. You can tell which is which on the plastic packet, as the salted version contains only salt, while the sweet contains salt and sugar. This type of preservation makes the mustard green almost herbal in flavour; slightly but not unpleasantly medicinal. This is a classic Hakka dish – the sweetness of the pork belly fat mellows it all out a bit, and makes you return to it with your rice bowl repeatedly. This type of mustard green tends to be very gritty, so don't skimp on the preparation process.

MUI CHOI PORK BELLY

SERVES
6
WITH OTHER DISHES

Rub the pork belly slices with the dark soy sauce and the five-spice and set to one side.

Rinse the mui choi well. Bring a large saucepan of water to the boil over a high heat, plunge the mui choi into the water and blanch for 3 minutes, stirring a few times. Drain, rinse with cold water and leave to soak in cold water for 20 minutes. Drain well, then cut the leaves into 1cm (½in) lengths and the stems into 5mm (¼in) lengths.

Heat the cooking oil in a wok on a medium heat and fry the pork belly slices, skin side down first, then on both sides, for a minute. Remove to a heatproof bowl, arranging the slices skin side down. Stir-fry the mui choi in the remaining fat in the wok until some of the residual moisture has dried out, then add the ginger, garlic and star anise and stir-fry for a minute. Remove and place on top of the pork belly slices.

In a measuring jug, mix the hot water with the rice wine, light soy sauce, oyster sauce and rock sugar until the sugar has dissolved. Pour this over the mustard greens in the bowl. Cover the bowl with foil or an appropriate lid and steam in a pan with a steamer insert or on a wire rack in a wok over a medium heat for 2 hours. Top up the water if it's running dry.

To serve, place a large plate over the bowl and very carefully turn the bowl over on to the plate so that the pork belly sits on top of the mustard greens. Serve with plenty of steamed white rice and other vegetable side dishes.

700g (1lb 9oz) pork belly, skin on, sliced into slices as thick as 2 fingers

1 tbsp dark soy sauce

pinch of five-spice powder (*see page 205 for homemade*)

150g (5½oz) sweet mui choi (*see page 162*)

150g (5½oz) salty mui choi (*see page 162*)

1 tbsp cooking oil

3 slices of fresh root ginger, about 2cm (¾in) thick, peeled and finely chopped

6 garlic cloves, very finely chopped

2 star anise

300ml (10fl oz/½ pint) hot water

1 tbsp Shaoxing rice wine

1 tbsp light soy sauce

1 tbsp oyster sauce

20g (¾oz) yellow rock sugar or white caster sugar

➤➤OTHER IDEAS
You can also mix the mui choi into minced meat and steam it, like a Chinese meatloaf.

I don't know when mu shu pork became so popular with American Chinese restaurants, but the same can't really be said for ones in the UK (in my experience). I hadn't heard of it before I bought a packet of dried lily buds on a whim, but my research told me that it was a classic ingredient of the dish, so in it went. This meal has been a staple for a while now; when I'm feeling over-indulged or I'm just after a lighter meal, it comes to my rescue. Our American friends might be perplexed by the lack of pancakes in this, but I find the crunch of the Little Gem leaves far superior – after all, if you want pancakes, roast duck is the only thing to stuff them with.

MU SHU PORK

SERVES 4

Mix the light soy sauce, water, rice wine and cornflour in a bowl. Add the pork and stir well to coat, then set aside to marinate while you prepare the other ingredients.

Drain the lily buds and tie each into a knot – this is to prevent them from breaking up when you are stir-frying. Heat 1 tablespoon of the cooking oil in a wok and swirl it around until just below smoking. Pour the beaten eggs in and leave to set as a round disc. You may need to scramble the centre and put the lid on to allow more heat to reach the rest. Once the egg has set, remove it from the wok and put to one side. Leave to cool for 5 minutes, then roll it up and slice it thinly.

Wipe the wok clean and heat the remaining tablespoon of oil over a medium heat until it is shimmering. Add the onion, garlic and ginger and stir-fry for 1 minute until fragrant and the onion is softening. Increase the heat to maximum and immediately add the pork, cabbage, bean sprouts, carrot, mushroom and the lily buds. Stir-fry constantly on the highest heat for 3–5 minutes until the pork is cooked and the vegetables are starting to soften. Add the slices of omelette and stir to combine.

Take the pan off the heat, drizzle in the sesame oil and garnish with the spring onion. Place in a serving dish with the Little Gem leaf cups for people to spoon the pork mixture into.

1 tbsp light soy sauce

1 tbsp water

1 tsp Shaoxing rice wine

1 tbsp cornflour

100g (3½oz) boneless pork shoulder or fillet, cut into thin strips

25g (1oz) dried lily buds *(see page 162)*, soaked in just-boiled water for 20 minutes

2 tbsp cooking oil

2 free-range eggs, beaten with a pinch of salt

1 small onion, sliced into half-moons

2 garlic cloves, very finely chopped

1 tsp peeled and grated fresh root ginger

100g (3½oz) Savoy or sweetheart cabbage, leaves separated and thinly sliced

100g (3½oz) bean sprouts

1 carrot, peeled and julienned

1 dried cloud ear or wood ear mushroom, soaked in just-boiled water for 15 minutes, then drained and julienned

1 tsp sesame oil

1 spring onion, thinly sliced diagonally

1 head of Little Gem lettuce, leaves separated and washed, to serve

The joy of these buns is in their fried bottoms. Steamed buns can at times be a bit too pillowy and sweet; in frying these, they become crunchy with a fluffy top. In my eagerness to eat them, I invariably burn my mouth and dribble pork juices down my chin. At least it's never dull.

PORK PRESERVED VEGETABLE BUNS

For the dough:

200g (7oz) strong white flour, plus extra for dusting

100g (3½oz) plain flour

1 tsp fast-action dried yeast

2½ tbsp sugar

1 scant tsp salt

2 tbsp cooking oil

175ml (6fl oz) water

For the filling:

3 leaves of Chinese cabbage (Chinese leaf or Napa cabbage)

1 tbsp fine salt

50g (1¾oz) Tianjin preserved vegetable (*see page 162*

2.5cm (1in) slice of fresh root ginger, peeled

1 spring onion

280g (10oz) fatty minced pork (fat is important here, as you want the insides to be juicy)

2 tsp light soy sauce

2 tsp sesame oil

1 tsp sugar

pinch of ground white pepper

1 tsp cornflour

1 tbsp cooking oil, plus a little extra for frying a sample of the filling to check the seasoning

For the dipping sauce:

1 tbsp Chinkiang black vinegar

½ tbsp water

pinch of sugar

1 tbsp chilli oil

Combine all the ingredients for the dough, except the water, in a mixing bowl, then add the water bit by bit until you get a soft dough, mixing thoroughly. Knead by hand on a lightly floured work surface, or using an electric mixer fitted with a dough hook, for 5 minutes until smooth. Put it back into the bowl, cover it with clingfilm and leave to rise in a warm place for an hour.

While the dough is rising, make up the filling. Slice the cabbage leaves in half lengthways and chop finely. Add to a colander and sprinkle with the fine salt. Leave over a bowl or the sink for 20 minutes for all the water to drain out.

Meanwhile, add the preserved vegetable to a large bowl of water to rinse some of the salt out. Leave this for 20 minutes too.

Chop the ginger and spring onion very finely and add to the pork with the soy sauce, sesame oil, sugar, pepper and cornflour. Mix with chopsticks in one direction until all is well amalgamated.

Rinse the cabbage and drain well, then add to the pork mixture. Rinse the preserved vegetable and chop roughly, then also add to the pork. Mix together well. Fry a teaspoonful of the mixture in a little cooking oil in a nonstick frying pan and taste to check the seasoning.

Tip the risen dough on to a floured work surface. Knead lightly a couple of times, then roll into a sausage shape and cut into 12 even pieces.

Press down on each piece of dough to form into a rough circle.

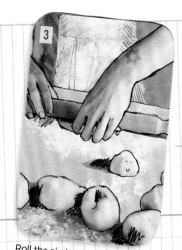

Roll the circle out to the size of your palm. It's preferable to have the middle a little thicker than the edges.

Add about a tablespoon of filling to each circle.

Then start gathering in the sides of the dough.

You should end up with a neatly sealed bun. Place the buns on a floured plate while you make the rest.

Twist until you have sealed the bun. Give the seal a pinch to ensure it's properly closed.

To cook, heat the oil in the nonstick frying pan and fry the buns flat side down. When the bottoms are browned, add a few splashes of water and put the lid on to steam them. Repeat a couple of times for about 8 minutes until cooked through. While the buns are steaming, mix the dipping sauce ingredients together in a serving bowl. Serve the buns hot with the dipping sauce.

Shaved thinly, sour bamboo shoots have a very particular smell of a musky pickled-ness that, though not unpleasant, does have a tendency to linger, and they need soaking to remove some of their saltiness. This simple Thai red curry is fragrant with basil, but is also sweeter than usual to counteract the acidity of the bamboo shoots.

SOUR BAMBOO SHOOT CURRY

SERVES 2

Soak the sour bamboo shoots in a large bowl of water for 30 minutes to get rid of some of the saltiness, then drain.

Heat the oil in a saucepan or wok over a medium heat. Add the coconut milk and bring to a simmer, then stir in the curry paste and simmer for 5 minutes. Add the sour bamboo shoots and simmer for 20 minutes, then slide in the hake fillets and lime leaves and simmer gently for another 5 minutes (or more, if your fish is thicker) until the fish is cooked through. Taste before adding the fish sauce, as the shoots can still be quite salty. Add the sugar to balance, take off the heat and throw in the Thai basil leaves. Squeeze the lime wedge over as garnish, stir and serve immediately with rice.

200g (7oz) sour bamboo shoots (*see page 163*)
1 tbsp cooking oil
400ml can coconut milk
2 tbsp Thai red curry paste
2 hake fillets
5 kaffir lime leaves
1 tbsp fish sauce
1 tsp palm sugar
handful of Thai basil leaves
wedge of lime, to garnish

Your friends, and even you, will probably baulk at the look of this dish – admittedly, transparent black egg whites and greenish-grey yolks aren't exactly appealing. But century eggs are really very mild in flavour and actually very pretty with this garnish. At least they'll be a talking point.

SERVES 4–6

AS A STARTER OR SIDE

CENTURY EGG SALAD

2 century eggs (*see page 163*)
1 large red chilli
1 large green chilli
1 spring onion
2 tbsp soy sauce
½ tbsp Chinkiang black vinegar
½ tsp sugar
a few fresh coriander leaves

Tap the eggs all over with a teaspoon and shell them carefully (submerging them in water makes the shell come off more easily). Halve each of the eggs, then place on a serving plate.

Deseed the red and green chillies and very finely chop them with the spring onion. Scatter this mixture over the egg halves.

Mix the soy sauce, vinegar and sugar together until the sugar has dissolved. Pour over the egg halves, and garnish with the coriander leaves.

These century eggs are fried until they're crisp on the outside, with slightly gooey centres. The star of the show here, though, is the chicken, so it's worth making this even if you can't find the blackened eggs. Sweet, salty, a little spicy and sour, the basil leaves give the dish fragrance, and it's quick to make.

SERVES 2 WITH OTHER DISHES

THAI FRIED CENTURY EGGS *with* CHICKEN

2 tbsp cooking oil, or more if needed

large handful of Thai basil (Italian basil works too), leaves plucked off the stems and divided equally into 2 piles

2 century eggs (*see page 163*), shelled (*see method on page 176*) and quartered

2 garlic cloves, very finely chopped

1 bird's eye chilli, roughly chopped

1 boneless, skinless chicken breast, roughly minced by hand

½ tsp sugar

1 tbsp fish sauce

1 tbsp oyster sauce

1 tbsp light soy sauce

¼ lime

Pour the oil into a wok and set over medium heat. Fry half the basil leaves for about 45 seconds until crisp. Remove and place on a plate lined with a piece of kitchen paper.

Next, fry the egg pieces, turning them so that they are cooked on all sides, for at least a minute each side until they are crisp. Remove and set them aside on a plate.

Place the wok back over medium heat, add the garlic and chilli, with a dribble more oil if it's a bit dry, and stir-fry for 2 minutes. Add the minced chicken, sugar, fish sauce, oyster sauce and soy sauce and stir-fry until the chicken is completely cooked, which shouldn't take more than 5 minutes in total.

Finally, stir in the rest of the Thai basil leaves until they are slightly wilted, then remove the chicken mixture to a plate. Arrange the fried century eggs around it, and sprinkle the fried basil leaves on top. Squeeze juice from the lime quarter over and serve with steamed rice and a couple of other dishes.

Oh wibbly, wibbly joy. This dish celebrates all three types of egg: preserved, salted and fresh. The preserved and salted eggs add flavour; the fresh gives it the body. Special care should be taken when steaming to avoid overcooking, as that would be a sad thing indeed. You're aiming for a just-set, panna cotta-like wobbliness. Eaten with some plain rice it is the ultimate comfort food, and you can customize the flavourings as you see fit; maybe fried minced pork flavoured with ginger, or add chopped marinated uncooked prawns halfway through the steaming process to finish off cooking in the egg.

STEAMED EGG CUSTARD with CENTURY and SALTED EGGS

SERVES
2
WITH OTHER DISHES

Set up a metal or bamboo steamer ready to go.

Crack the fresh eggs into a bowl and whisk with a fork. Add hot water (which should be a comfortable temperature when you stick a finger in it) using each of the eggshells – you want a ratio of 1:1.5 egg to water, so use each half once and 2 halves once more. Whisk again. Pour through a sieve into a heatproof dish that is small enough so that the mixture is at least 5cm (2in) thick – the sieve gets rid of the foam of the egg, which would make a bubbly surface.

Shell the century egg (*see method on page 176*) and dice into pieces, then crack the salted egg, discard the egg white and chop the yolk in half. Scatter these into the egg mixture.

Cover with clingfilm and place inside the steamer. Steam for 8 or so minutes over a high heat, checking all the while. You want wobble but not liquid.

Meanwhile, slice the green part of the spring onion diagonally. Mix the soy sauce with the sesame oil and water.

When the egg custard has set, remove from the heat and pour the soy sauce mixture over, then garnish with the spring onion greens. Serve immediately.

4 free-range fresh (chickens') eggs
1 century egg (*see page 163*)
1 salted egg (*see page 163*)
1 spring onion, green part only
1 tbsp light soy sauce
1 tsp sesame oil
½ tbsp water

This really is a dish to dive into with your hands, possibly wearing a bib. The luxurious combination of the salted egg yolks and butter flavours the evaporated milk (don't use condensed – there's quite an important difference) with the delicate aroma of the curry leaves. Rip the heads off the prawns, suck the head juices out, lick your fingers and repeat. You may need a wash afterwards.

SALTED EGG BUTTER PRAWNS

SERVES 2

1 large red chilli
1 small red chilli
3 salted egg yolks (*see page 163*)
50ml (2fl oz) cooking oil
8 uncooked tiger prawns in their shells
25g (1oz) butter
2 garlic cloves, lightly crushed but leaving them whole
10 fresh curry leaves
3 shallots, finely sliced
75ml (2½fl oz) evaporated milk
½ tsp sugar

Chop the large chilli roughly, and cut a slit in the small chilli but leave it whole. Add the egg yolks to a small heatproof bowl and steam in a metal or bamboo steamer over a high heat for 10 minutes until cooked. Leave to cool a little, then mash with the back of a spoon.

Heat the cooking oil in a wok on a high heat until it shimmers. Add the prawns and stir-fry for 1 minute so that they're half-cooked. Remove and drain on kitchen paper. Drain off the rest of the oil, reserving 1 tablespoon.

Add the butter and garlic cloves to the wok and stir-fry for 2–3 minutes over a medium heat until fragrant. Add the curry leaves and red chillies, followed by the shallots, and stir-fry to combine for 1 minute, then stir in the salted egg yolks. Add the evaporated milk and sugar and simmer for 5 minutes.

Add the prawns back in, coating with the sauce and moving them around until they're fully pink and cooked, which should only take a couple of minutes. Dish out on to a serving plate and serve with plenty of napkins.

You'll often find fermented white tofu (bean curd) flavoured with sesame oil or chilli, and you can use either kind in this recipe instead of plain.

SUGAR SNAP PEAS, SCALLOPS & BABY CORN *with* WHITE FERMENTED TOFU

SERVES 2

Heat the cooking oil in a wok on a high heat until just below smoking and sear the scallops on each side for about 30 seconds until they have a golden brown crust. Remove and set to one side.

Add the baby corn to the wok and stir-fry for a minute on a high heat, then add the garlic, sugar snap peas or asparagus, tofu, soy sauce and rice wine with the water. Stir-fry constantly for about a minute until the vegetables are almost tender. Add the scallops back in and carefully turn over a few times, then take the pan off the heat. Serve with the spring onion placed on top, with steamed rice.

1 tbsp cooking oil

8 large shelled scallops, preferably with roes attached

100g (3½oz) baby corn, cut in half, then in half again lengthways

1 garlic clove, very finely chopped

150g (5½oz) sugar snap peas, or green asparagus, woody tips snapped off and cut into 7.5cm (3in) lengths

2 cubes of white fermented tofu (bean curd) (*see page 163*), mashed with a fork

1 tsp light soy sauce

1 tsp Shaoxing rice wine

50ml (2fl oz) water

1 spring onion, julienned

This is a Cantonese classic, eaten on hot rice with a drizzle of roasting juices. The red fermented tofu (see page 163) is crucial for the right flavour, and is indeed great to marinate or stew any meat for a deeper, more intensely savoury flavour.

CHINESE ROAST PORK BELLY

If your piece of pork belly has bones, remove these so that the slab sits as level as possible. If the skin hasn't been scored, do so with a very sharp knife but only the skin, not through the fat to the flesh.

Place the piece of pork belly on a rack in the sink and pour a full kettle of just-boiled water carefully, slowly and evenly over the skin of the belly in the sink. Leave to drain and dry.

Mix the fermented tofu with the five-spice, 1½ teaspoons of salt, the sugar and garlic. Dry the piece of pork belly with kitchen paper and place on a plate, skin side down. Score the flesh about half the depth of the meat into wide strips (so perhaps 3 times), then rub the marinade over the pork belly meat and into the cuts. Turn back over, dry the skin, rub with 1 tablespoon of salt and leave to marinate in the fridge, uncovered, for a minimum of 4 hours or overnight.

Take the pork belly out of the fridge about an hour before cooking so that it can come up to room temperature, wiping the salt off the skin. Preheat your oven to 220°C (425°F) Gas Mark 7, rub the skin with a little cooking oil and place the pork on a rack in a roasting tin, skin side down. Pour enough boiling water into the roasting tin to cover the bottom of it, but not so that it touches the pork. Roast for 25 minutes, then turn over and roast for a further 30 minutes. (If your piece of pork belly is bigger than 1kg/2lb 4oz, roast for 20 minutes per 450g/1lb of the total weight plus 20 minutes.)

Remove the pork from the oven and leave to rest for 15 minutes. If the skin isn't crisp or hasn't puffed up much, place under a hot grill, and watch it like a hawk, for a few minutes until it has puffed.

To serve, chop the pork into thick slices or bite-sized pieces. Fan out on a plate for everyone to help themselves with a small bowl of Homemade Sriracha (see page 109) for dipping.

800g (1lb 12oz) piece of pork belly with skin (boneless weight)

2 cubes of red fermented tofu (bean curd) (see page 163), mashed with a fork

½ tsp five-spice powder (see page 205 for homemade)

salt

1 tsp sugar

2 garlic cloves, grated on the finest setting of a box cheese grater

cooking oil, for rubbing

Homemade Sriracha (see page 109), to serve

CHAPTER

SPICES &DRIED VEGETABLES

SPICES & DRIED VEGETABLES

A huge part of Asian supermarkets is taken up by the dried goods. The Chinese probably use more dried goods than the other Asian cuisines; their earthy dried mushrooms are used not only to flavour stews, but in salads and to provide additional texture, while five-spice powder and star anise spices are essential flavourings for particular dishes, usually involving meat. You may notice after your wanderings at the supermarket that I haven't included any traditional Chinese medicinal herbs; that's mainly because getting into that lot would be a whole new book. And it's better to stick to things that taste nice...

(1, 2, 3, 4 & 5) STAR ANISE, CASSIA BARK, CINNAMON STICK, CUMIN, FENNEL & CURRY SPICES

These are the spices used mostly in braising or marinating meats. The southern parts of China use a lot of star anise (1), cassia bark (2) and cinnamon (3), while the northern parts such as Xinjiang use cumin (4) and fennel (5) more.

FIVE-SPICE POWDER

A common spice mix, usually consisting of star anise, cloves, cinnamon, Sichuan peppercorns and fennel seeds, used in braising. You can buy this in most supermarkets (check the label as some brands include salt), or make your own (*see page 205*).

(6) CHILLIES & SICHUAN PEPPERCORNS

There are different types of dried chilli, but most common are the bell shaped, romantically named 'heaven-facing chillies', and the long, thin chillies. Sichuan peppercorns (6) are a joy themselves for their unique ability to make your mouth go a little numb.

1.

2.

3.

4.

5.

6.

7.

8.

9.

10.

11.

(7 & 8) MUSHROOMS

Shiitake (7) are the most commonly available type of dried mushroom, but you will also come across cloud ear and wood ear mushrooms (8).

SEAWEED

The Japanese use wakame seaweed, sold dried, mostly in salads and soups. Kombu is sold as large sheets for you to cut up and use to flavour stocks like dashi (see page 209). Nori comes in sheets, which are paper thin and used as wraps for sushi and onigiri (rice balls), but can also be toasted until crisp, crumbled into flakes and used as a seasoning or garnish. Purple seaweed, usually sold dried in discs, is used solely for Chinese soups.

(9, 10 & 11) DRIED TOFU (BEAN CURD)

This is made by skimming the surface of soya milk in production to lift off the top layer of skin, much like what you may have experienced on top of your school canteen custard, which is then dried into a variety of shapes and formats to suit different preparations. Tofu bamboo (9) are sticks of dried skin gathered up; tofu skin (10) (called yuba in Japanese) are flat, dried sheets which can sometimes be scrunched up a little, while tofu knots (11) are, as you might suspect, tofu skin tied into knots. Dried sheets of tofu are usually used for sweet dessert soups, while tofu sticks are a little sturdier, reserved

for stews. Tofu knots are often added to soups and stews for additional texture, and they also retain the juices within the knot, creating a flavoursome mouthful. Tofu bamboo is commonly used in salads. In all cases, dried tofu needs to be rehydrated before use.

DRIED FLOWERS & FRUITS

Dried chrysanthemum flowers are used to make tea (see page 210), and dried goji berries can flavour dishes or be a flavouring in their own right (see page 210).

GINKGO NUTS

Ginkgo nuts are usually sold in cans or vacuum packed. Eaten most commonly at special occasions, such as Chinese New Year or weddings, they are often eaten with congee or desserts, and are said to have health benefits.

RED ADUKI (AZUKI) BEANS

Sold as dried beans, ready cooked in cans or mashed and sweetened into a paste, red aduki beans are used most frequently in desserts.

This is, undoubtedly, a bit of a gnarly one. Fish HEAD? You mean, I have to eat a head? Well, yes. Sorry. But fish do have heads, and heads happen to be really quite delicious. Especially that nugget of cheek just under the eyes – it's soft and smooth, silky and tender. If you have any really brave friends, they might be up for eating the actual eye. Alternatively, you can make this with fish fillets – you'll just need firm, white fish, preferably with skin to hold it together. You might recognize a lot of the spices in this dish from Indian cookery, as Malaysian cuisine is an intriguing mix of Chinese and Indian influences.

MALAYSIAN FISH HEAD CURRY

SERVES 2

1 fish head – ask your fishmonger for this; red snapper, hake and cod are all good, but avoid oily fish like salmon

1 tbsp sea salt flakes

1 tbsp cooking oil

1 tbsp tomato purée

400ml (14fl oz) can coconut milk

100ml (3½fl oz) water

1 tsp sugar

8 okra, halved widthways

3 tomatoes, quartered

½ tsp salt

½ lime, for squeezing

leaves from 2 sprigs of fresh coriander, to garnish

For the spice paste:

1 onion, roughly chopped

5 garlic cloves, roughly chopped

2.5cm (1in) piece of fresh ginger root, peeled and roughly chopped

2.5cm (1in) piece of fresh galangal root, peeled and roughly chopped

½ tbsp coriander seeds, toasted and ground

1 tsp chilli powder, or to taste

1 tsp ground cumin

½ tsp ground turmeric

1 tsp fennel seeds, toasted and ground

1 tbsp cooking oil

Rub the fish head with the sea salt flakes and set aside.

Blend all the spice paste ingredients together in a blender to a fine paste.

Heat the cooking oil in a wok over a medium heat until it is shimmering and fluid. Add the spice blend, turn the heat down low and fry for 10 minutes, stirring often. Add the tomato purée, coconut milk, water and sugar, then stir well so that everything is combined. Simmer on a medium heat with the lid off for 15 minutes. Add the okra and simmer for a further 5 minutes.

Rinse the salt from the fish head, then add to the wok so that it is submerged in the sauce. Add the tomatoes around the fish head, then put the lid on and simmer gently for 15 minutes (less if using fillets), turning the fish head once during this time. Season with the salt and spoon out into a deep serving dish. Squeeze over the lime juice, garnish with the coriander leaves and serve with rice.

20 dried heaven-facing (bell-shaped) chillies

3 slices of fresh root ginger, peeled

2 tbsp Sichuan peppercorns

1.2 litres (2 pints) chicken stock

1 tsp salt

170g (6oz) (about half a 340g block) firm tofu (bean curd), cut into chunks

300g (10½oz) skinless coley fillet, cut into chunks

2 spring onions, diagonally sliced

SICHUAN FISH *and* TOFU HOTPOT

SERVES 4

WITH OTHER DISHES

Sichuan peppercorns have the glorious ability to make your mouth tingle and become numb when you eat them. They have a slightly metallic, citrus tang to them, and after a big Sichuanese meal I often find myself craving more. This is probably the spiciest recipe in the book. It looks the part, with a vast sea of chillies bobbing about in the broth, but you're not supposed to eat them; they're there to flavour, not to annihilate. The romantic-sounding chillies are called 'heaven facing', as apparently that's what they look like they're doing.

Add the chillies, ginger and Sichuan peppercorns to the stock in a saucepan and simmer for a good 40 minutes with the lid cocked. Add the salt and the tofu chunks for the last 10 minutes of the cooking time.

Finally, add the fish to the broth and take off the heat. Leave to stand for 10–15 minutes with the lid on to cook the fish through. Garnish with the spring onions and serve. Instruct your guests to fish out the tofu and the coley, spooning minimal broth on to lots of steamed white rice as they go.

Katsu curry is often regarded as the junk food of Japan, and since we're breading and deep-frying meat before smothering it in sauce, I'm not really in a position to refute that. But although it is the antithesis of Zen-like sushi and miso soup, it is still a wonderful thing in its own right; the curry sauce is mild and sweet, fragrant and silky against the crisp meat. It is unchallenging, warming and is everything you want in a comfort dish.

CHICKEN KATSU CURRY

SERVES 4

2 boneless, skinless chicken breasts, sliced in half lengthways

4 tbsp plain flour, seasoned generously with salt and pepper

1 free-range egg, beaten

2 handfuls of panko breadcrumbs

200ml (7fl oz) cooking oil

For the sauce:

1 tbsp cooking oil

1 onion, diced

4 garlic cloves, very finely chopped

2 carrots, peeled and roughly chopped

1½ tbsp medium curry powder

1 heaped tbsp plain flour

600ml (20fl oz/1 pint) chicken stock

2 dessert apples

1 tbsp light soy sauce

1 tsp sugar

Place the chicken breast halves between 2 sheets of clingfilm and lightly bash them with a rolling pin to thin them out a bit to a uniform thickness. Set aside and repeat with the rest of the chicken.

Heat the cooking oil for the sauce in a large saucepan and fry the onion over a gentle heat for 10 minutes until soft and translucent. Add the garlic and fry for 3 minutes, then stir in the carrot. Add the curry powder and the flour and stir well to combine, then whisk in the stock gradually to avoid lumps. Peel, core and grate the apples into the saucepan and finally add the soy sauce and sugar. Simmer gently on a low heat for 30 minutes.

Preheat the oven to 110°C (225°F) Gas Mark ¼. Place the seasoned flour on a plate and the beaten egg on another plate or in a shallow bowl. Have a third plate for the panko breadcrumbs. Pour the cooking oil into a wok or saucepan large enough to accommodate the chicken breasts and heat to 180°C/350°F, or until bubbles appear up the sides of a wooden chopstick when inserted into the hot oil. Then dip the chicken, one piece at a time, firstly in the flour, then in the egg and finally in the breadcrumbs before slipping into the hot oil. Fry for 4 minutes on each side, turning over if the oil doesn't cover the chicken. Remove to a rack set over a baking sheet and place in the oven while you fry the rest of the chicken.

Cut each piece of chicken into 3 slices and serve with the sauce and steamed rice. You can pass the curry sauce through a sieve on to the rice if you like, but actually I like all the bits of vegetable, so I rarely bother with the sieve.

➤➤OTHER IDEAS

Use the curry sauce as a sauce for chips, a posh version of what you get at the fish 'n' chip shop.

Spiced nuts aren't a new or unusual idea, but I particularly like these for the build-up of that numbing feeling as you're chowing down. These cashews are the perfect beer snack; spicy, salty and incredibly addictive.

SERVES
2
AS A
SNACK

SICHUAN PEPPERCORN CASHEWS

1 tbsp cooking oil
½ tsp fine sea salt
1 tsp chilli flakes
1 tsp Sichuan peppercorns, toasted and finely ground
200g (7oz) unsalted raw cashew nuts

Preheat the oven to 160°C (325°F) Gas Mark 3. Line a baking sheet with nonstick baking paper.

Combine the oil with the sea salt, chilli flakes and half the ground Sichuan peppercorns. Add the nuts and toss well so that they are coated in the mixture. Spread them out in a single layer on the lined baking sheet and roast for 15 minutes, turning a couple of times so that they are cooked evenly.

Remove from the oven and leave to cool for 5 minutes, then place in a bowl and sprinkle with the remaining Sichuan pepper.

This curry is classic winter food, though often eaten for breakfast; beef cooked until soft and almost collapsing in a spiced and thick sauce. I love the inclusion of both potato and mooli (daikon), an alternating bite between creamy stodge and the crisper, cleaner 'turnip'. The Vietnamese still have a lot of culinary tradition derived from the French colonization, and this is reflected in the baguette that is often served with it to dip in the sauce.

BO KHO
(VIETNAMESE BEEF CURRY)

SERVES 4

If using the annatto seeds, heat the cooking oil in a frying pan, add the seeds and cook over a medium heat for 5 minutes, then remove from the heat and set aside until cool. Sieve the annatto seeds out of the oil.

Toss the diced beef with the flour and fry in the annatto oil (or plain cooking oil) in a large saucepan until browned. Add the onion, garlic, ginger and lemon grass, and stir to combine. Fry for another 3 minutes before adding the star anise, curry powder, coriander, fennel, five-spice powder and cinnamon stick. Mix well and fry for a further 5 minutes on a low heat.

Add the canned tomatoes, plus a can of water. Simmer gently over your lowest heat, uncovered, for 2 hours, stirring every so often. If it's looking dry, add a little more water. Then add the carrots, mooli and potato, and simmer for about 40 minutes.

Add the fish sauce, stir to combine and taste, then add more if it needs it. Serve with a hunk of baguette or some rice to soak up the sauce.

2 tbsp cooking oil

2 tbsp annatto seeds (optional)

700g (1lb 9oz) shin of beef, or any other slow-cooking beef, cut into bite-sized pieces

4 tbsp plain flour

1 onion, roughly chopped

5 garlic cloves, squashed with the side of a knife

5cm (2in) piece of fresh root ginger, peeled and very finely chopped

2 lemon grass stalks, chopped in half

3 star anise

1 tbsp medium curry powder

1 tsp ground coriander

1 tsp fennel seeds, toasted and ground

1 tsp five-spice powder (*see page 205 for homemade*)

1 cinnamon stick

400g (14oz) can chopped tomatoes

2 carrots, peeled and roll cut (*for method, see page 153*)

1 small mooli (daikon), peeled and roll cut (*for method, see page 153*)

4 floury potatoes, washed and chopped into 4

1 tbsp fish sauce, or to taste

This is a minimal-effort dish, but one that brings a high reward. Especially popular with children, the cola reduces down to a sticky and addictive glaze. If you use other chicken portions, it will be inferior; you really need the finger-licking quality that wings bring to it. I'm not saying it's good for you, but once in a while...

SERVES 4 WITH OTHER DISHES

COLA CHICKEN WINGS

800g (1lb 12oz) chicken wings

2 tbsp dark soy sauce

3 garlic cloves

2 spring onions

2 tbsp vegetable oil

3 slices of fresh root ginger, peeled

1 star anise

2 tbsp light soy sauce

1 can of cola (not diet or flavoured)

drizzle of sesame oil

Joint the chicken wings – they are usually in 3 segments, and you want to separate the middle bit from the fleshier end (not the wing tip). Place in a bowl and rub with the dark soy sauce. Leave to marinate for a few minutes, and while doing so, crush the garlic and separate the white and green parts of the spring onions, chopping the whites roughly and slicing the greens diagonally.

Heat the vegetable oil in the wok and brown the chicken pieces well. Remove and set aside. Stir-fry the garlic, ginger and whites of the spring onions with the star anise. Add the chicken wings back in, stir to coat and add the light soy sauce. Open the can of cola and pour into the wok. Bring to the boil, then let it simmer for 20 minutes. It may not quite cover the chicken pieces, in which case turn the pieces over and simmer for a further 20 minutes. By this point the sauce should have reduced to become thick and glossy – if not, simmer for a bit longer.

To serve, place on a serving dish and garnish with the spring onion greens. Drizzle with the sesame oil and serve with steamed white rice and a vegetable side dish or two (*see page 84*).

This is the kind of dish that is made for winter. The star anise works beautifully with beef, and you'll find that your whole house smells aromatic and a little spicy, while you tap your foot, impatiently waiting for it to do its cooking thing. Cuts of beef that work particularly well are anything with some fat on it or connective tissue so that it all breaks down with the slow cooking into a delicious, lip-smearing, beefy hug. I sometimes use half ox cheek and half beef tendon (see page 156 for cooking instructions) for a little textural contrast.

RED-BRAISED OX CHEEK

SERVES 4 WITH OTHER DISHES

Bring a saucepan of water to the boil and blanch the ox cheek pieces in the boiling water for 2–3 minutes. Drain and rinse the ox cheek pieces, and rinse the pan out. This is to get rid of the scum that clouds the broth. Place the ox cheek pieces in a clay pot (see page 11) or a snug saucepan.

Heat the cooking oil in a wok and stir-fry the chilli bean paste with the ginger, garlic and spring onion whites. Add the yellow bean paste and rice wine, then the star anise and the stock or water. Bring to the boil and add to the ox cheek. Put a lid on it and braise very slowly for 3–4 hours until the ox cheek is tender. Top up with a little water (or stock if it didn't all fit) if it's looking dry.

Serve, garnished with the spring onion greens, on rice or on noodles.

450g (1lb) ox cheek or other beef for slow cooking, cut into bite-sized pieces

2 tbsp cooking oil

2 tbsp chilli bean paste (see page 16)

20g (¾oz) fresh root ginger, peeled and thinly sliced, then whacked with the side of a knife

3 garlic cloves, slightly crushed

2 spring onions, white parts only, chopped into 7.5cm (3in) pieces, green parts reserved and sliced

1 tbsp yellow bean paste (see page 16)

2 tbsp Shaoxing rice wine

1 star anise

500ml (18fl oz) beef stock or water

My favourite restaurant in London, Silk Road, makes these lamb skewers with chunks of pure lamb fat interspersed with the meat; they become crispy and juicy once grilled over intense heat. As soon as they put the plate down on the table, hands come out of nowhere grabbing at them. I have, on many occasions, tried to solicit some sort of recipe out of the guys there, but to no avail. This is as close as I've got – it's something of a different beast, as it works with a wet marinade rather than a dry spice rub, but it is pretty great nonetheless. Lamb fat optional.

SERVES 4

XINJIANG LAMB SKEWERS

650g (1lb 7oz) boneless lamb shoulder

2 tbsp cumin seeds

1 tsp Sichuan peppercorns

5cm (2in) piece of fresh root ginger, peeled and very finely chopped

4 fat garlic cloves, very finely chopped

3 tsp ground cumin

pinch of salt

3 tbsp chilli bean paste (*see page 16*)

4 spring onions

Chop your lamb shoulder up into cubes and put into a bowl.

Toast the cumin seeds in a dry frying pan on a medium heat for a couple of minutes until you can smell their aroma, shaking the pan often to stop them catching. Leave to cool, then grind with a pestle and mortar, or spice or coffee grinder if you have one. Do the same with the Sichuan peppercorns.

Add both spices to the lamb along with the ginger, garlic, cumin and salt and mix well, then add the chilli bean paste. Cut the spring onions into 2.5cm (1in)-long sections, add to the lamb and mix together. Cover the bowl with clingfilm and leave to marinate in the fridge for a few hours or overnight. Meanwhile, if you don't have metal skewers, presoak some wooden ones in water for a good 30 minutes (but even so, beware of them catching fire; metal are better).

Take the lamb out of the fridge a couple of hours before cooking so that it comes up to room temperature. Thread the lamb on to your skewers, alternating with the spring onion. Cook over a hot barbecue or a smoking hot griddle pan on the hob for a few minutes each side so that they are charred and cooked through but not burned. Serve with a cooling salad.

Quail might well be my favourite (edible) bird. Their tiny bodies don't take long at all to cook and, provided you use a high heat, you are well rewarded with crisp skin and juicy meat that you can eat a little pink. It may also be to do with feeling like a giant, ripping off those teeny-weeny drumsticks.

FIVE-SPICED QUAIL

SERVES 4 WITH OTHER DISHES

4 oven-ready quails

2 garlic cloves, peeled

½ tsp salt

1 tbsp clear honey

2 tsp five-spice powder
(*see below for homemade*)

1 tsp dark soy sauce

½ tsp Sichuan peppercorns, toasted and finely ground

2 tbsp cooking oil

1 lime, cut into wedges

Spatchcock your quails. Do this by first placing a quail breast side down on your chopping board and removing any trussing bands that might be holding its legs together. Then cut lengthways along the centre of the underside of the quail with a sharp knife, turn the quail breast-side up and push the breastbone down with your palm to flatten it.

Using a pestle and mortar, roughly bash the garlic with the salt. Add the honey, five-spice, soy sauce, Sichuan pepper and 1 tablespoon of the oil and mix together well. Rub this mixture over the quails in a shallow dish, cover the dish with clingfilm and leave to marinate in the fridge overnight.

Take the quails out of the fridge a couple of hours before cooking so that they come up to room temperature. Preheat the oven to 200°C (400°F) Gas Mark 6. Heat the remaining tablespoon of oil in a heavy-duty, cast-iron or nonstick frying pan over a medium heat. Add the quails (if you can fit them all in the same pan) skin side down and fry them for 5 minutes, pressing down on them with a spatula all the while so that they cook evenly and the skin becomes crisp. Once bronzed, flip them over, then transfer to a roasting dish and roast for 10 minutes. Serve with lime wedges.

MAKES

1 SMALL JAR

You will notice that there are six spices in my five-spice. I'm a rule breaker. These spices are all available to buy whole and cheaply at the Asian supermarket.

DIY FIVE-SPICE POWDER

Toast all the spices in a dry frying pan on a medium heat for around 3–4 minutes until they are aromatic, shaking the pan often. Leave to cool, then grind in a spice or coffee grinder. Keep in an airtight container.

20g (¾oz) star anise

20g (¾oz) fennel seeds

20g (¾oz) cassia bark

15g (½oz) Sichuan peppercorns

10g (¼oz) black peppercorns

1 tsp cloves

This is a homely, comfort-food type of dish. The oyster sauce, chicken flavours and mushroom juice meld together to make an addictive, slightly sweet sauce that you will almost abandon the chicken for just to spoon it over white rice. The mushrooms soak up the sauce too, so that every time you bite into one, a great gush of juices is released into your mouth. Truly, the chicken plays second fiddle here. Don't forget the rock sugar; I've made this recipe so many times, wondering what was missing, and it was that.

SERVES 2

BRAISED CHICKEN, BROCCOLI and SHIITAKE MUSHROOMS

1 tbsp Shaoxing rice wine

1 tbsp light soy sauce

½ tsp ground white pepper

3 skinless chicken thighs on the bone, each chopped into 3 pieces through the bone – you can ask your butcher to do this, or do it yourself carefully with a sharp cleaver

2 tbsp cooking oil

5 thin slices of fresh root ginger, peeled

5 garlic cloves, very finely chopped

10 dried shiitake mushrooms, soaked in cold water overnight then drained

1½ tbsp oyster sauce

150ml (5fl oz/¼ pint) water

2 tsp or 1 small lump of yellow rock sugar

1 spring onion

6 broccoli florets

1 tsp cornflour, mixed with **2 tbsp** cold water

Mix the rice wine, soy sauce and white pepper together in a bowl. Add the chicken thigh pieces, turning to coat well, cover with clingfilm and leave to marinate in the fridge for at least an hour – overnight is ideal, but the dish won't suffer too much if it's a shorter period of time.

Heat the oil in a wok on a high heat until it is shimmering but not smoking. Stir-fry the ginger slices and garlic until fragrant, then add the chicken plus its marinade and stir-fry until it has lost a bit of its rawness and taken on some colour.

Cut off the mushroom stems using a pair of kitchen scissors and add the mushrooms to the wok, along with the oyster sauce, water and the rock sugar. Stir to combine, then add the lid and braise on a low heat for 30–45 minutes. Or you can decant the mixture to a clay pot (*see page 11*) to braise, freeing your wok up to cook vegetables or another dish.

Slice the white of the spring onion into 7.5cm (3in) lengths, then cut in half lengthways. Add to the pan or pot along with the broccoli florets, put the lid back on and cook for a further 5 minutes, still on a low heat. Test the broccoli for tenderness – if it's still a little firm, give it a couple of minutes more.

Add the cornflour solution to the pan or pot, mixing well. When the sauce thickens and becomes glossy (usually within about a minute), the dish is ready. Carefully tip upside down on to a plate so that the chicken and mushroom mixture lies on top of the broccoli. Slice the greens of the spring onion finely and scatter on top to serve.

5 dried cloud ear or wood ear mushrooms, soaked in just-boiled water for 15 minutes, then drained

1 large carrot, peeled and julienned

50g (1¾oz) blanched shelled broad beans or peas

3 tofu bamboo sticks (*see page 189*), soaked in just-boiled water for 30 minutes

1 large red chilli, sliced into thin rings (optional)

1 spring onion, sliced into 7.5cm (3in) lengths and very thinly sliced lengthways

1 tbsp rice vinegar

1 tsp salt

2 tsp sesame oil

½ tsp sugar

SERVES 4 AS A SIDE

CLOUD EAR FUNGUS and TOFU BAMBOO SALAD

This salad is a great combination of textures: the cloud ear mushrooms are crunchy and a little slithery, while the tofu bamboo is smooth and silky, and slightly chewy. It's a pretty plate of spring colours, and you can add or substitute other vegetables like peppers, blanched broccoli or roasted cauliflower into the mix.

Chop the mushrooms so that they are still quite large but discard the tough core. Place in a bowl with the carrot and the broad beans or peas.

Drain and squeeze the tofu bamboo gently, then rip roughly into 3. Add to the mushrooms. Throw in the sliced chilli, if using, and the spring onion.

Whisk the rice vinegar with the salt, sesame oil and sugar, then toss the vegetables with it. Serve immediately.

This is an incredibly traditional Chinese soup, made using discs of purple seaweed called zi cai (or zhee choi in Cantonese). I haven't found any other use for this type of seaweed other than in soups, and when suspended in liquid it has a throat-sweeping, silky texture as it goes down. I find it very soothing. If you can't find clams, substitute them with mussels, thinly sliced white fish, soft silken tofu (bean curd) or chicken.

SERVES 2

PURPLE SEAWEED EGG DROP SOUP

700ml (1¼ pints) chicken stock

1 tsp peeled and very finely chopped fresh root ginger

1 tbsp Shaoxing rice wine

4 small chunks of loofah gourd (*see page 82*) (optional)

10g (¼oz) dried purple seaweed, soaked in cold water for 10 minutes

400g (14oz) live clams, scrubbed clean

pinch of ground white pepper

1 free-range egg, beaten with **2 tbsp** light soy sauce

1 spring onion, green parts only, shredded

Place the stock in a saucepan with the ginger, rice wine and the loofah gourd, if using, then bring to a gentle simmer and cook for 3 minutes.

Drain the purple seaweed and add this with the clams and pepper. Place the lid on the pan and simmer for a further 3–5 minutes until the clams have opened. Discard any that do not open.

Take the pan off the heat and, while stirring the soup gently in one direction, pour the beaten egg in so that the strands are suspended in the liquid. Top with the spring onion greens and serve with an additional bowl for the discarded clam shells.

piece of dried kombu (*see page 188*), about 16cm x 20cm (6¼in x 8in)

1 litre (1¾ pints) water

handful of dried bonito flakes

Place the kombu and water in a large saucepan and leave for 10 minutes. Bring to the boil, and just as it boils, remove from the heat. Add the bonito flakes and leave to sit for 10–15 minutes, then strain through a fine sieve to use.

MAKES

ABOUT 1 LITRE
(1¾ PINTS)

HOW TO MAKE DASHI

Dashi is the backbone of Japanese cuisine. You can buy it in powdered form, but it is so easy to make that I prefer to do so myself. From here you can mix it with white miso paste to make miso soup, and use it for simmering liquids and noodle broths. It is also often used in dipping sauces. There are a few different types of dashi – one involves shiitake mushrooms, called shiitake dashi, but there is also niboshi dashi, made by pinching the heads off dried baby sardines and using them to flavour the stock. But the most commonly used is kombu dashi, made with katsuaboshi, which are dried bonito flakes – shavings from a dried, smoked skipjack tuna. You can buy them in big resealable bags.

≫►OTHER IDEAS

Dried bonito flakes are often placed on top of noodles, noodle soups or savoury pancakes called okonomiyaki – the steam from the food makes them look like they're waving or dancing.

When I was a kid, my mother used to boil a load of dried chrysanthemum flowers in water to make a tea, sweetened with yellow rock sugar. I was told that this tea is particularly good for you when you've eaten too much fried food, and it helps clear your complexion. Whether or not that is true, it's still a delicious drink, floral and mildly herbal; a perfect coolant during hot summer months.

CHRYSANTHEMUM TEA

SERVES 4

50g (1¾oz) dried chrysanthemum flowers
1.5 litres (2¾ pints) water
30g (1oz) yellow rock sugar

Wash the chrysanthemum flowers in a sieve and add to the water in a large saucepan. Bring to the boil, then simmer on a very gentle heat for 5 more minutes.

Take the pan off the heat and stir in the rock sugar, then leave to cool. Strain through a fine sieve and drink either cold or at room temperature.

Goji berries, sold dried, plump up to become soft and sweet in this herbal tea. You can have this hot or cold.

GOJI BERRY LEMON TEA

SERVES 1

1 tbsp dried goji berries
1 black tea or Earl Grey tea bag, or of your choice
1 slice of lemon
honey, to taste

Wash the dried goji berries and place in a mug. Add the tea bag of your choice and pour boiling water over it. Leave to steep for 1 minute, then use a teaspoon to squeeze the remaining water out of the tea bag.

Leave for 5 minutes so that the goji berries hydrate. Add the slice of lemon and honey to taste.

For a while, goji berries were hailed as a 'superfood', and started appearing in the mainstream. But the Asians have been eating them for years; steeped in teas, dessert soups and savoury dishes. They are sweet and inoffensive, a welcome splash of colour to what could otherwise be a dreary plate. This dish has no danger of appearing dreary – there's a lovely ceremony to bringing a whole fish to the table for people to pick at with chopsticks.

STEAMED BREAM with GOJI BERRIES

SERVES 4 WITH OTHER DISHES – 2 AS A MAIN

Preheat the oven to 200°C (400°F) Gas Mark 6. Lay a large sheet of foil in a roasting tray, then line the bottom of the foil with nonstick baking paper. Scatter over half the matchsticks of ginger, then place your fish on top. Cut 2 slits at right angles to the spine of the fish through the flesh and scatter the goji berries on top. Drizzle the water around it. Gather up the sides, rolling and crimping to make a tight seal so that no steam escapes. Place in the oven to steam for 13–15 minutes (13 for a small/medium bream or bass, 15 for a larger fish). The flesh should come away from the bones easily.

Remove the fish from the foil and carefully lift on to a serving plate, taking the goji berries with it but discarding the ginger and pouring off any liquid that has accumulated. Top with the spring onions and the remaining ginger.

Meanwhile, heat the cooking oil up in a small saucepan for a couple of minutes on a medium heat so that it is just below smoking. Leave to cool for 20 seconds, then very carefully tilt the oil away from you and pour in the light soy sauce, dark soy sauce, sesame oil and sugar. It may splatter, so stand away from it. Swirl and stir to combine, then pour over the fish.

Serve with other vegetable sides (*see page 84*) and some plain steamed rice.

5cm (2in) piece of fresh root ginger, scraped clean of skin and sliced into very thin matchsticks

1 whole sea bream or sea bass, gutted and scaled

2 tbsp dried goji berries

3 tbsp water

2 spring onions, sliced into 10cm (4in) lengths and julienned

2 tbsp cooking oil

2 tbsp light soy sauce

1 tsp dark soy sauce

1 tsp sesame oil

1 tsp sugar

The Asians use red aduki beans as a dessert ingredient, either mashed into a paste or whole, for soups, ice creams and fillings. When I was growing up, I loved the ice lollies you could buy from the shops flavoured with nutty, creamy sweetened red beans that coloured them a dramatic reddish purple; you could also get olive-green mashed green mung bean versions. You can buy sweetened red bean paste at the Asian supermarket, but I prefer to make it myself so that I can control the texture and the sweetness.

RED BEAN ICE LOLLIES

MAKES 4–6 DEPENDING ON YOUR MOULD SIZE

Open the can of beans and drain the water out of it, or drain the cooked dried beans. Remove 3 heaped tablespoons of the beans and set to one side. Put the rest of the beans into a saucepan with the coconut milk, sugar and salt and simmer on a gentle heat for 15 minutes without the lid.

Leave to cool for 10 minutes. Using a stick blender, blitz until smooth. Pass the mixture through a fine sieve. Add the reserved beans back into the mixture, then spoon into 4–6 ice-lolly moulds. Freeze for at least 4 hours. To eat, dip each lolly mould in hot water for 10 seconds to release the lollies from the moulds.

400g can aduki beans in water
or **200g dried** aduki beans, soaked in cold water overnight then drained and simmered in 1 litre (1¾ pints) fresh water for 1 hour or until soft
350ml (12fl oz) coconut milk
5 tbsp sugar
pinch of salt

Black sesame ice cream is dramatic; grey-black in appearance, it often draws startled gasps from dinner guests who haven't seen it before. I like adding berries to a bowl of this ice cream, but served with the sesame honeycomb, this is a flavour bomb. The honeycomb is also good eaten just as it is, with coffee.

BLACK SESAME ICE CREAM *with* BLACK *and* WHITE SESAME HONEYCOMB

SERVES 4

Whisk the egg yolks with the sugar in a bowl until they become creamy.

Toast the black sesame seeds in a dry nonstick frying pan on a medium heat for a minute or two until they become fragrant. Do not let them burn. Leave to cool, then grind finely using a spice or coffee grinder if you have one, or a pestle and mortar.

Add the ground sesame seeds to the milk in a large saucepan, then add the cream. Heat until it comes to just under boiling, which will take about 3 minutes. Watch it like a hawk. Then take the pan off the heat.

Add the vanilla and leave to infuse for 30 minutes in a cool place. Add a few spoonfuls of the milk mixture to the egg mixture and stir well. Keep adding the milk mixture until all is incorporated, then put back on a low heat, stirring and heating until it has thickened – do not let it boil. It should resemble custard.

Strain the sesame seeds out and put the mixture in the fridge to cool thoroughly before churning/freezing in an ice-cream maker according to the manufacturer's instructions. Alternatively, you can leave the mixture to set in a freezer-proof container in the freezer and freeze for a couple of hours until almost frozen, then use a stick blender or transfer to a blender to break down the ice crystals, though you will then have to repeat the process 3–4 times until the ice cream is frozen to avoid any lumps of ice.

To make the black and white sesame honeycomb: Toast the sesame seeds in a dry frying pan over a medium heat for about 5 minutes until browned and fragrant but not burned, mixing often. Set aside. Line a large baking sheet with nonstick baking paper so that the paper overlaps the sides amply.

Heat the sugar and golden syrup in a large, heavy-based saucepan (you'll see why you need a large one later) over a low heat, stirring occasionally, until the sugar has melted into liquid form. This will take about 10 minutes. Turn the heat up to medium and bubble for 7 minutes until a deep amber colour but not any darker. Take off the heat immediately and add the toasted sesame seeds and vanilla extract, stirring well. Then add the bicarbonate of soda and mix quickly. At this point the mixture will bubble and froth; spoon it quickly on to the lined baking sheet and leave to set. Get your saucepan into hot water as quickly as you can, before the caramel sets on to the pan. Fill with boiling water if needs be to re-melt the sugar residue.

Leave the honeycomb to cool for 2 hours, then break into pieces – it tends to break randomly, so if you want neat pieces, use a serrated knife in a sawing motion. Store in an airtight container and eat within a couple of days, or dip each piece entirely in melted chocolate and it will keep pretty much indefinitely.

For the ice cream

2 free-range egg yolks

85g (3oz) caster sugar

7 tbsp black sesame seeds

350ml (12fl oz) semi-skimmed milk

200ml (7fl oz) whipping cream

1 tsp vanilla extract

For the honeycomb

40g (1½oz) white sesame seeds

40g (1½oz) black sesame seeds

200g (7oz) caster sugar

6 tbsp golden syrup

½ tsp vanilla extract

2 tsp bicarbonate of soda

It might seem odd to have a soup for dessert, but it's very common in Cantonese culture and this is a particularly classic one. The tofu (bean curd) becomes soft and willowy, flavouring the soup to resemble soya milk. This, like many soups, has a basis simply of water sweetened with yellow rock sugar (which the Chinese believe is good for the lungs), called tong sui in Cantonese. I can't say this will be to everyone's taste, but it's certainly a change from Western-style desserts. If this is a bridge too far for you, you can also make savoury soups and stews with the tofu skin.

CANTONESE BEAN CURD SKIN DESSERT SOUP

SERVES 4

1 litre (1¾ pints) water

30g (1oz) pearl barley, washed

2 sheets of dried tofu skin *(see page 189)*, broken into pieces with your hands and soaked in cold water for 10 minutes

3 fresh pandan leaves, tied in a knot

60g (2¼oz) yellow rock sugar

30g (1oz) ginkgo nuts *(see page 189)*, from a vacuum pack or a can

Bring the water to the boil in a large saucepan with the pearl barley, tofu skin pieces and the pandan leaves. Simmer for 30 minutes.

Remove the pandan leaves and discard. Add the rock sugar and ginkgo nuts and simmer for another 10 minutes. Serve warm or cold.

Dim sum can often consist of steamer upon steamer of intricately pleated dumplings, where the skill of a deft touch and a lightness of hand is needed to make them. These meatballs, however, are far more forgiving and easy to make. Here, the tofu bamboo works as a protection against the meatball sticking to the plate, but it also soaks up all the juices released from cooking.

STEAMED BEEF BALL DIM SUM *with* TOFU BAMBOO

SERVES 4 AS A STARTER OR SNACK

Dice the lard into very small pieces and add to the minced beef in a bowl, then add all the remaining ingredients, except the tofu bamboo and Worcestershire sauce. Mix with your hand, folding the meat over and squeezing gently for about 5 minutes, until it becomes well combined and sticky. Leave for 30 minutes to marinate.

Mix again for another 5 minutes, then gather it up in your hands, giving it a squeeze, and slap hard back into the bowl or on a clean work surface. Repeat 10 times. This gives the characteristic 'bouncy' texture once steamed.

To cook, line a plate with a lip with the tofu bamboo straightened out into sheets and place in a metal or bamboo steamer. Arrange the steamer in a wok half-filled with boiling water (not enough so that it touches the steamer). Roll the beef into 10 balls each around 4cm (1½in) in diameter and place on the plate. Put the lid on and steam in the wok on a high heat for 10 minutes. At this stage you can split one in half to check whether it's cooked through; if not, steam for another 3 minutes.

Drizzle with Worcestershire sauce before serving.

30g (1oz) lard
200g (7oz) minced beef
1 tsp grated orange rind
1½ tbsp oyster sauce
½ tsp ground black pepper
1 tsp peeled and grated fresh root ginger
small handful of fresh coriander, very finely chopped
½ tsp bicarbonate of soda
1 tbsp cornflour
½ tsp salt
1 tbsp sugar
40g (1½oz) drained canned water chestnuts, roughly chopped into small pieces
1 spring onion, very finely sliced
4 tofu bamboo sticks (*see page 189*), soaked in just-boiled water for 15 minutes
2 tbsp Worcestershire sauce, to serve

INDEX

ACKNOWLEDGEMENTS

Thanks firstly go to my awe-inspiring agent, Diana Beaumont. Thank you to Mitchell Beazley and the team for putting this together - Yasia, Stephanie, Sybella - you're all great. Thank you for the belief in my idea, thank you for your patience and hard work. Thank you David, Tab, Annie and Abi for making it look just how I wanted it to, and more.

I'd like to thank my parents, Hazel and Peter, for having the good sense to meld their genes together. Credit too goes to them for bringing me up to be such a greedy person, always looking forward to my next meal and always planning my circumstances around something delicious. It is a special skill honed through the privilege of being a Mabbott.

To my enduring friends and housemates, Emily, Luke and Chris. For all the washing up, for stuffing yourselves silly and eating all that weird shit I put upon you. I made you trim the nails from chickens' feet. I made you gut chickens. You put tripe in your mouths unwillingly. I am grateful.

Big thanks also to EuWen, Cherry, Melon & Donald, Nicola and Adam for helping me out in my time of need. I'd also like to thank Naz and Jane for being awesome creative gurus, and to Joe, for the wonderfully conditional support. Thank you, Macca, for the killer fruit facts, and to James, for the opportunity.

Finally, a huge thanks to Stevie for being my sounding board, my strategist, my jar of self belief, my guinea pig, my wine pusher, my cheerleader. I'd be a jibbering wreck if it weren't for you. I'll never force coconut creme patissiere on you again.